NEITHER
CIVIL
NOR
SERVANT

Published by
Straits Times Press Pte Ltd
Singapore Press Holdings
Mezzanine Floor, Information
Resource Centre
Level 3, Podium Block
1000 Toa Payoh North, News Centre
Singapore 318994
Tel: (65) 6319 6319 Fax: (65) 6319 8258
stpressbooks@sph.com.sg
www.stpressbooks.com.sg

STRAITS TIMES PRESS

General Manager   Susan Long
Publishing Manager   Lee Hui Chieh
Creative Director   Lock Hong Liang
Marketing and
Operations Manager   Ilangoh Thanabalan
Sales Manager   Irene Lee
Book Editor   Audrey Yow

Proofreader   Fong Siew Chong

Printed in Singapore
First printed in October 2016
Reprinted in December 2016, and
March, April and July 2017

**National Library Board, Singapore
Cataloguing-in-Publication Data**

Name(s): Peh, Shing Huei | Han, Fook
Kwang, author. | Straits Times Press Pte.
Ltd., publisher.
Title: Neither civil nor servant: the Philip
Yeo story / Peh Shing Huei with
Han Fook Kwang.
Other title(s): Philip Yeo story.
Description: Singapore: Straits Times Press
Pte Ltd, [2016]
Identifier(s): OCN 958358808 | ISBN
978-981-4642-63-7 (paperback) | ISBN
978-981-4642-71-2 (hardcover)
Subject(s): LCSH: Yeo, Philip, 1946– |
Singapore—Officials and employees—
Biography.
Classification: DDC 352.63092—dc23

Straits Times Press

NEITHER CIVIL
NOR SERVANT

THE
PHILIP
YEO
STORY

PEH SHING HUEI

with

HAN FOOK KWANG

CONTENTS

FOREWORD

George Yeo (second from right) at the groundbreaking ceremony
of Biopolis with Philip Yeo (second from left) in 2001.
Source: Singapore Press Holdings

I have known Philip Yeo since our school days. He was a classmate of two of my brothers at St Joseph's Institution, and a senior to another two of my brothers at the University of Toronto. As a young officer in the Singapore Armed Forces (SAF), I was a staff officer to him when he was the Second Permanent Secretary of the Ministry of Defence (Mindef). After he left Mindef to become Chairman of Economic Development Board (EDB), we continued to keep in touch. When I became Minister for Trade and Industry, he was co-chairman at EDB and chairman of the Agency for Science, Technology and Research (A*STAR). Both statutory boards came under my responsibility. Under his leadership, Singapore's biomedical sciences sector flourished. When Kerry Logistics, a company I chair, was listed on the Hong Kong Stock Exchange at the end of 2013, I persuaded Philip to become one of my independent non-executive directors. We remain very close friends. In some ways, we share a kindred spirit.

He is people-centred, task-oriented and decisive. He evokes in many of his subordinates a fierce loyalty. Among them, he is usually referred to as "chairman". I enjoyed working for him. When a submission was put up to him, he would decide quickly, rarely asking for further study or clarification. Clarity is important especially for a large organisation like Mindef. One day, when Philip was in Mindef during the early 1980s, he summoned me to his office. I was Head of Air Plans in the Republic of Singapore Air Force (RSAF) then. Singapore should purchase four E2C Hawkeye tactical airborne early warning aircraft from the US. Could I write the staff paper to make the recommendation to Mindef HQ? I duly did, never fooling myself that the decision taken was the result of any argument I made.

Philip looks after his staff and takes a personal interest in their welfare and families. I have never seen him seek advantage for himself. He was happy that some of the people who worked for him earned significantly more than he did. He would always take care to visit scholarship students and junior staff when he travelled and take them out to dinner, which was invariably Asian. Of course, he expected them to serve their duty and became justifiably upset when scholarship holders broke their bonds without good reason.

Once he embarks on a mission, he is unstoppable. Philip works best when he enjoys the full support of his superiors. In Mindef, he received full backing from Goh Keng Swee and Howe Yoon Chong, both of whom were Minister for Defence from 1970 to 1979 and 1979 to 1982 respectively. Without Philip, Singapore's defence industries, from which a number of our government-linked companies had their origins, would not have made such rapid strides. As Chairman of EDB, he took Singapore's economy to a new level. Jurong Island was his baby. As Chairman of A*STAR, he built up the biomedical sciences sector and put it on the world map. When he took on the responsibility of A*STAR, he restocked his shelves with books on biomedical sciences. Never pretending to be an expert, he quickly knew enough to seek out the right people and ask the right questions.

I remember how the Genome Institute of Singapore (GIS) was established. We were having lunch at my office in the Ministry of Trade and Industry not long after the first draft of the Human Genome Project came out in June 2000. I mooted to Philip the possibility of building a facility for Singapore. He was thinking along the same lines. Once he got the green light from me, he sped off like an F1 driver to recruit Dr Edison Liu and proceeded to get the Institute off the ground. When SARS hit us in February 2003, we would have been much worse off without the Institute's initial sequencing capability.

Having little patience for bureaucracy, Philip naturally has his detractors. It does not help that Philip is not a politician. Indeed, he has no patience for politics and speaks his mind freely, sometimes too freely. He dismisses some bureaucrats as "useless", others as "bean counters". When I was Minister for Trade and Industry, some of his criticisms were directed at ministers and Members of Parliament. I defended him as best I could and also counselled him to be more measured in his public statements. He sensed being increasingly sidelined by the government and, at one point, seriously considered a rather lucrative offer from Hong Kong to join the private sector.

One night, I received a telephone call from Lee Kuan Yew (then Senior Minister) asking me whether he should speak on behalf of Philip to the Cabinet. He knew that Philip could be "insubordinate" but said that his contacts among global CEOs and his ability to break new ground were nonpareil. I agreed wholeheartedly and supported Lee Kuan Yew's personal intervention. It was a huge relief to me because I knew what a loss it would have been to Singapore. Great men have their rough edges.

Philip is constantly on the move, constantly absorbing new knowledge, constantly helpful to those who seek his support. In or out of government, whether in my role as subordinate, superior, peer or friend, he has never refused my request for assistance. His attitude is that he would contribute if he could, provided the person who asks is sincere and the cause is worthwhile.

This book by Peh Shing Huei sketches an accurate, vivid portrait of Philip Yeo, and describes his inimitable qualities as an atypical civil servant and as a wonderful human being. Readers will, like me, marvel at Philip's energy level and can-do spirit. They will also appreciate why his counsel is sought all over the world by those who see in the Singapore system an inspiration for themselves, and how Philip Yeo is a personification of Singapore's positive traits.

George Yeo

INTRODUCTION

Philip Yeo.
Source: Economic Development Innovations Singapore (EDIS).
Photographer: Kua Chee Siong

As Jonathan Kua walked up to a restaurant in Harvard Square, he was told by Philip Yeo to wait outside the eatery. It was unusual. Yeo, his boss, usually included him and other Economic Development Board (EDB) officers in all meetings and meals. "I knew it was a special conversation," recalled the young staffer. He stood outside the restaurant at Cambridge, Massachusetts, and waited. "Our loyalty to him was very deep," he said. "Whatever he said, we obeyed. We asked the questions later." Six months on, he would realise why he was not allowed into the private lunch on August 29, 1999. It was a rendezvous between high-flying EDB chairman Yeo and Richard Li, son of Hong Kong billionaire Li Ka Shing. Li wanted the Singaporean to join his Singapore-based fund management vehicle Pacific Century as executive chairman. In the months that followed, after further secretive meetings in Britain, Hong Kong and Thailand, Li would table an eye-popping offer more commonly seen by film and sports stars than a nerdy civil servant.

Pacific Century would pay Yeo S$28 million over three years, which translated to a S$9.3 million annual package. It included a S$10 million signing-on bonus, S$10 million salary over three years and share options worth S$8 million. "It was a lot of money in those days," said Yeo's long-time aide Lai Chun Loong, who helped negotiate the package. It is still a lot of money today. Yeo was ready to end his 13-year association with EDB and three-decade long career as a civil servant in the Singapore government. In an e-mail to an old friend in December 1999, he wrote: "I've always had the 'itch' to try to make it in the private sector. Time is running out. Like what Elvis Presley sang, 'It's Now or Never'."

But it was neither now nor never. It just wasn't then. Yeo would set up his own firm, the Economic Development Innovations Singapore (EDIS) in 2013, plunging into the private sector as a bona fide entrepreneur. He never took up Li's offer. When Singapore's *The Business Times* newspaper got wind of the courtship, it broke the news in February 2000 that Yeo could join Li's firm in a "senior role". It cited an unnamed former colleague who said: "I hope he joins Richard Li. It will make him rich. But I suspect he will take up a non-executive position as I don't think the government will let him go. The man is a great asset to Singapore."

The Singapore government was indeed not prepared to release Yeo. Cabinet ministers worked behind the scenes to persuade him to stay, knowing the patriot was motivated by cause more than cash. He had famously said: "Money doesn't bother me. I'm not broke, I'm not rich, but I'm happy. So long as the work is fun and you're happy, just do it." When he ran the Singapore Technologies (ST) group, for instance, he diversified and listed the businesses without taking any shares and profiting from it. It was the same when he listed telco Pacific Internet, which was a billion-dollar company at one point. Yeo was keen to explore life sciences as the next frontier for Singapore's economy and the authorities knew the carrot could counter Li's millions. Yeo himself admitted in a personal e-mail to a friend that he was happy in the government. "Really have no complaints financially," he wrote. "My work is up to me to make and create. And I do enjoy the breadth of my work and it allows me to satisfy my curiosity in science matters." The clincher came when Singapore's founding prime minister Lee Kuan Yew met Yeo, expressed deep concern on his exit plans and personally asked him to stay. Said Yeo: "I couldn't say no to him." Pacific Century's offer was put on moratorium, with Li and Yeo agreeing that the latter could take up the job any time he was ready. He never did.

While Yeo mentioned the Pacific Century offer in his farewell speech from the Agency of Science, Technology and Research (A*STAR) in 2007, the details of the offer were never shared publicly until now. The quantum tabled was, and still is, a private sector offer which few, if any, Singapore civil servants could command. But Philip Yeo was not a normal civil servant. He likes to say that he was neither civil nor servant. He was also not in favour of rules, hierarchy, red tape, due process, meetings, memos and pretty much everything associated with bureaucracy. He was a businessman in a bureaucrat's skin, a salesman more than a servant and a public official who belonged to the private sector. In more ways than one, he was a walking contradiction tap dancing through contrasting terrain in a colourful 40-year public service career. He has never written an aide memoir in four decades. As an elite Administrative Service officer for 29 years, he had never submitted a Cabinet paper. "Don't call me a civil servant. I consider that an insult," he said.

There are few neutral observers when it comes to Philip Yeo. He divides opinions. Fans hail him as a brilliant leader who inspires devotion, is not afraid to lead from the front and get his hands dirty, pointing to his long list of accomplishments from industrialising Batam to creating the Jurong Island. Critics denounce him as an arrogant civil servant who once told an elected Member of Parliament to resign, and has little appetite for contrarian views. Allies praise him for being patient, nurturing and loyal. Rivals slam him for being combative, defiant and egoistic. "He does things in a way which many people find too direct, too linear, and he's prepared to rock the boat which many people find uncomfortable," said former Cabinet Minister George Yeo, an old friend and former colleague. "And he sometimes speaks, one might

13

say, perhaps too bluntly... I'm not surprised that there are people who think poorly of him."

A rare label which most could agree on was "maverick". "Great leaders are usually divisive," said Goh Song How, who worked with him in the Ministry of Defence and Sembcorp. "People either hate Philip Yeo or they love Philip Yeo. He's a one of a kind civil servant. I can't even see a second one close to him." Love him or hate him, there is no denying he was "one of Singapore's most accomplished and colourful government officials", as mentioned in *The Business Times*. Tycoon Kwek Leng Beng, who helms the Hong Leong Group Singapore, said Yeo "is never afraid to take the contrarian view". Yeo sits on the board of City Development Limited, a property subsidiary of Hong Leong. "He is constantly pushing boundaries and looking at areas where things can be improved," added Kwek. "He is plain-spoken, shares his thoughts and allows room for criticism and debate."

At his prime, he was also regarded as one of Singapore's sexiest men. In 1991, he was named by local *Her World* magazine as one of Singapore's 25 sexiest men. Yeo, said the magazine, "is a living example that you don't have to score an A in looks to be sexy".

For such a maverick, controversies were inevitable, even though he was ensconced in the opaque world of the civil service. He was not afraid to challenge naysayers publicly, regardless of status and background. When MP Chng Hee Kok disagreed with his move to publicly name scholarship bond breakers, he told him to resign from Parliament. In 1999, when Yeo was running Pacific Internet, he clashed openly with Singtel, whose CEO was Lee Hsien Yang, younger son of Lee Kuan Yew. Yeo had called Singtel a "sugar daddy" to its division Singnet, accusing it of subsidising Singnet. In 2007, he would take on Lee Kuan Yew's daughter Lee Wei Ling when she openly questioned his work in the biomedical sciences sector. When a blogger criticised A*STAR's scholarship scheme, Yeo sparred with him online.

And those were just the more memorable contests which spilled into the public domain. The feisty Yeo had many more bouts, fought and settled privately. "There were sharp clashes in the bureaucracy because there were permanent secretaries and others who felt that he was not conventional, that he disliked meetings," said George Yeo. "Civil servants have long meetings and every time they are unsure they ask for more data, more studies. Really, the doubts are in them. It's not that the data would flush out those doubts, they just don't want to decide, so they go round and round in a circle, frustrating everybody along the way... Philip's very impatient about meetings." A local tabloid, *The New Paper*, called him "Mr Controversy". "He is someone who does what he says and says what he means," said EDB director of human resource Ng Ying Yuan. "We don't see many leaders who behave that way."

Unlike most senior civil servants, or many Singapore public figures for that matter, Yeo is famously candid. Said current EDB chairman Beh Swan Gin, who was a young officer under Yeo: "He is prepared to be very upfront with his views and would say it as it is without sugarcoating it." At times, Yeo seems almost incapable of being politically correct. Former EDB director of human resource Khoo Seok Lin said: "Before every press conference, we had to beg him 'Chairman, please behave, okay?' It was impossible to control him." His delivery was often in rapid fire mode, with the safety catch turned off. He frequently referred to those whom he has a dim view of as "idiots". To him: "Dummies are still adorable. Idiots are hopeless." He once said that those with only basic degrees in the biomedical sciences sector would be test-tube washers. Former EDB officer Chia Hsin-Ee recalled that her friends in

15

the industry, who were biology graduates, were livid about that comment. "They were all saying, 'why is Philip Yeo saying this? Does it mean that I have no future and I'm going to be a test-tube washer?'," she said. "Then I went into the life science industry and I realised actually it was true that those with basic degrees wash test tubes. He was stating the facts in a very in-your-face way."

Part of his straight talking ways is a result of his intensely driven and passionate personality. "Yeo seems to operate on perpetual fast-forward, an intense, impatient and driven man who said he would die of boredom if asked to relax," said *Asia Times* in a profile in 1996. "He speaks so fast that his mouth often struggles to keep up with the rapid flow of instructions sent by his brain. Elegant grammatical structures give way to a machine-gun style of communication, sentences being overwhelmed by a torrent of ideas, some thoughts overtaken in mid-flow by more pressing messages."

16

In the interviews for this book, Yeo, who turned 70 in 2016, rarely stayed on topic. Straying off course became par for the course after a few sessions. For instance, a discussion on Biopolis would quickly move to the Greek island of Lesbos. An exchange on drawing investments somehow morphed into a chat on iTunes apps. Random thoughts would pop into his head – why the Dutch are tall (they eat cheese); his dream home (shaped like a mushroom, surrounded by books); how nuns are more prone to breast, ovarian and uterine cancers (risks increase with the number of menstrual cycles) – and became part of the interviews, peppered liberally with colloquial Singapore English, or Singlish, Chinese dialects and the odd Malay words. He often created his own words, such as "*chabot-ed*", the past tense of the Malay word "*chabot*", which means to run away.

Once, after we became more familiar with each other, I asked him if he has ADHD – Attention Deficit Hyperactivity Disorder. He laughed and said: "Maybe! Maybe!" Edgar Schein, a Massachusetts Institute of Technology management professor who wrote a book on the EDB, said: "Philip Yeo is undoubtedly one of the fastest thinking and fastest moving managers I have ever met. (He's) an extremely dynamic, proactive individual who produces concepts, information and proposals for action quite rapidly and gets involved in projects at a very detailed level."

Such speed, dynamism and colour undergird this biography of Philip Yeo, a year-long project to cover almost half a century of public work. It covers industries he built, like defence, electronics, wafer fabrication, chemicals and biomedical sciences. It reaches far beyond Singapore, sharing adventures from Indonesia to China, from the United States to Japan. To tell this complex story, I referred to books, journals, newspapers and magazines in my research, in addition to Parliament records and archival materials. Yeo also gave ample access to his personal letters and e-mails, allowing insights which had hitherto been kept to a very select group of friends and long-time colleagues. He offered unprecedented access to his time and thoughts, with 10 interview sessions in his penthouse office in Fusionopolis, Singapore. These were topped with almost 40 interviews with people familiar with him, ranging from Cabinet Ministers past and present to senior civil servants, from top business leaders to scientists, from colleagues to childhood friends. Unless otherwise stated, all quotes in this book are from these interviews.

The book runs on two tracks – chronological and thematic. It adopts a broad chronological approach, tracing his life from childhood to university, from his early years in defence to his halcyon days as the economic czar of Singapore. But such is the complexity, even untidiness, of his career that neat divisions would not be possible. Yeo did not move from one job to another.

He frequently juggled a few at the same time. In the early 1980s, for example, he was second permanent secretary in the Ministry of Defence (Mindef), chairman of the new National Computer Board (NCB) and running a host of defence-related companies under the ST group. A timeline drawn of his career ended up with three parallel columns. Hence, the narrative is both chronological and thematic.

The biography has four sections. In the first, it explores the least-known side of Yeo, including his childhood, family, private life and years in school before he joined the civil service. The second part delves into his time in Mindef and the defence industries, a long association with the military, weapons and warfare of more than two decades which many Singaporeans have since forgotten. Many of the stories here had never been made public previously. The third section goes into his EDB adventures, a famous period when he became a near household name in his country and built a global network which some believed was among the best in the world. It culminated in the audacious Jurong Island project. The last segment of the book looks at his biomedical sciences story with Biopolis and A*STAR, his current work at EDIS, his management style and views on Singapore's current affairs and beyond. But in a career as long and diverse as Yeo's, some segments of his work, such as his time in NCB and Defence Science Organisation and his building of Bintan from jungle to tourist resort, had to be condensed in the interest of readability. This, after all, is a man with an encyclopedic resume.

There was never a dull moment in the interviews with Yeo and I hope I have captured adequately the exciting moments in the nine chapters of this book. Each chapter ends with an extract of the dialogue between myself, Han Fook Kwang and Yeo, which illustrates his fast speaking and irreverent style. Clearly, this is not the first, nor will it be the last, word on the maverick of the Singapore civil service. There will be those who remember the stories in this book differently. It is my intent that these pages provide an early draft in the story of Philip Yeo, a foundation for others to build on, assess and critique a public official who was neither civil nor servant.

Peh Shing Huei

PART I

Source: Wong Kok Seng

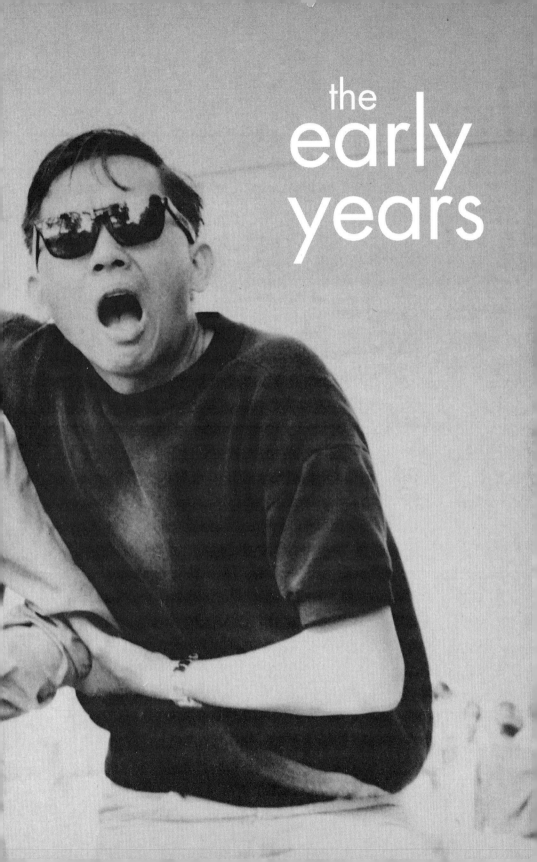

the
early
years

The Lone Ranger

*"Philip was a person
of few words in school."*

former St Joseph's Institution classmate Wong Kok Seng

As the GCE "A" Levels examinations drew closer, Philip Yeo was increasingly concerned about his impending chemistry grade. He could answer the written questions in the exam comfortably, but felt that he sorely lacked lab practice. His chemistry teacher had not been around for weeks and the rules of St Joseph's Institution (SJI) disallowed students from using the labs without a teacher.

"My classmates and I were all getting worried," he said. The exams were crucial. The grades would determine his eligibility for university entry and Yeo was gunning for a scholarship to study overseas, likely in Canada. The teenager badly needed some lab practice and decided to do something radical – he set up his own lab. He was living with his aunt in an old shophouse along Beach Road, by the seafront in southern Singapore, and he converted her attic into a make-shift chemistry lab.

However, he needed money to buy chemicals and equipment. To fund the self-built chemistry lab, Yeo turned to his extra-curricular activity in school, where he was in charge of audio and visual equipment. He would use the school projector to screen movies on campus every Saturday and charge an entrance fee. He explained his business plan to the vice-principal and was given the green light to start his cinema. Yeo and his classmates rented movie reels from local film company Cathay Organisation at S$25 per film and staged three screenings every Saturday at between 25 cents to 50 cents per ticket, open to the public. The first film he ran was *Run Silent, Run Deep*, a movie about submarine warfare starring Clark Gable and Burt Lancaster. It was a hit. "I made a lot of money. And my friends had fun selling movie tickets to the girls in CHIJ," he said with a laugh, referring to the all-girls Catholic school, Convent of the Holy Infant Jesus, across the road from SJI's compound at Bras Basah in downtown Singapore.

Flush with box office takings, he and his classmates bought bottles of flammable and corrosive chemicals from a shop at downtown Cross Street, including nitric acid, sulphuric acid and hydrochloric acid. "Our vice-principal gave us a letter authorising us to buy the chemicals. They were huge bottles. One of us would ride the bicycle and the other would carry the bottles. We never knew the danger," he said. A small fire in the house, recalled classmate Tan Guong Ching, ended the home lab. But the practice it gave to the SJI boys was sufficient. "Most of my classmates scored As for their chemistry," said Yeo. He managed a B and a string of As from other subjects and snagged a Colombo Plan scholarship to study industrial engineering at the University of Toronto in Canada. It came with a five-year bond to work in the Singapore government.

The fluid use of resources gave an early glimpse of Yeo's creative and maverick ways. "He exhibited that entrepreneurial streak even as early as in secondary school," said fellow SJI student Wong Kok Seng.

He is a man of action and believes in taking whatever steps necessary to reach his objective. "If you really want to get something done, you have to do it – by hook or by crook," Yeo said. When the school labs were not available, he built his own. When he needed money to build a lab, he started a campus cinema. The early successes would encourage him to morph into a master of flexibility and a prominent rule breaker in the civil service, an institution of laws, rules and norms. It would also shape him as an action figure, less given to pondering than practice. Unlike the film he screened, he was neither silent nor very deep. "He wasn't a great theoretician," said Richard Sykes, former chairman and CEO of pharmaceutical giant GlaxoSmithKline. "Philip Yeo was a doer." As Yeo loved to expound, he was no thinker. At best, he said he was a tinkerer. "I like to change things," he said. "To me, a thinker sits under a tree. A tinkerer is more important, like Leonardo Da Vinci. It's not that he didn't think. But he got things done too. I want to see results, I want to see a project, I want to see something tangible."

Few could have seen the future of Noel Philip Yeo Liat Kok in the early years after his birth in 1946, a year after the end of the Japanese Occupation in Singapore. He was the second of three children born into a poor migrant Teochew family, a people originally from southern Guangdong province in China with its distinctive dialect and cuisine. Before he turned four, his father died. Yeo knew little of his dad, except that he was Chinese-educated, worked with the Red Cross during the war and most likely had a deep affection for China. Yeo senior gave his second born the Teochew name "Liat Kok" or "Lie Guo" in Chinese. It means "passion for the country", and was a reference to China, not British colony Singapore. After all, Philip's brother was named "Liat Tong", or "passion for China". Yeo would be known by his Teochew name in his family and in St Anthony Boys' where he attended primary

school. "My mum, who passed away a few years back, called me 'Ah Kok',"
he recalled. "Ah" is a common prefix which most Chinese Singaporeans use
with names as a form of affection. At age 12, he was baptised as a Catholic
and was christened Noel Philip. He went with Noel, which was chosen by his
baptism godfather, for some years before settling on Philip when he entered
university. "Noel felt too Christmasy," he explained. Some old friends from
SJI still call him Noel.

The passing of his father affected the family severely. His elder brother
and younger sister were left in the care of his grandmother, while he followed
his mother on a nomadic lifestyle, moving from house to house while she
worked as a domestic helper for expatriate families. "We were very poor. We
had next to nothing," he said. "My father was gone, my mother was working. I
was left alone most of the time." The benign neglect worked out swimmingly
for Yeo. He entertained himself by climbing trees, catching spiders and
fishing for guppies in the monsoon drains. When his mother moved to work
in a house along Handy Road, near Cathay cinema in downtown Singapore,
he slipped into the theatre frequently without paying. "I waited till the movie
started and when no one was watching, I would go into the cinema," he said,
sticking out his tongue cheekily. "Sometimes, when there were empty seats,
I could even enjoy the movie sitting down."

The cinema also helped him earn extra pocket money. He recalled: "A
pair of sisters cordoned off a patch of land opposite Cathay and turned it
into a bicycle parking space. It wasn't their land but those were the days
when people could do whatever they wanted. Few people drove cars then.
Most rode bicycles. These two sisters charged people some 20 cents to keep
their bicycles and my job was to help park them. I got 5 cents per bike. It was

25

very good money. I loved it when there were big movie nights, like the Malay movie *Pontianak*. I learnt to be financially independent from a young age."

He also learnt to be socially independent. At SJI, he was quiet, well behaved and hardly noticed. "Philip was not that articulate and was a person of few words in school," said Wong. Yeo quickly realised he did not have a herd mentality. While most of his friends wanted to be prefects, he preferred the less prestigious and hardly sexy task of handling audio and visual (AV) equipment. "What's a prefect? He's a guard. He stood at the school gate, waited for latecomers and blacklisted them. No one liked prefects," he said. "I took charge of AV and I got the microphone ready for the principal to give his morning sermon every day. All the students had to stand in attendance to hear the lecture in the hot sun. I was happily sitting alone in the control room with my legs up. When people go this way, I go another way. Why should I follow the crowd? Whenever I was asked to do normal things, I died of boredom." His classmate said that was an early example of his leadership ways. "He always knew what needed to be done," said Tan Guong Ching. "He didn't like to be straight-jacketed with rules." As Yeo would say repeatedly of his youth: "I liked to be left alone to do my own things." During school holidays, he would hire a rowing boat, fill it with books and drift into the waters off Singapore's northeast coast on his own for a day of quiet reading. It was one of the rare luxuries he afforded himself. It is perhaps no surprise when he named the fictional character Lone Ranger as his childhood hero.

He found another sanctuary in school to be left in his own world – the library. He served as librarian during his six years in SJI, from Secondary 1 to Pre-University. "I had access to all the books first," he said, proudly. It would nurture a lifelong passion for books and reading. He amassed a phenomenal collection of books, journals, magazines and, curiously enough, beige-coloured laminated paper. His penthouse office in Fusionopolis has a personal library and the shelves are filled not only with books and journals, but also carefully labelled folders packed with beige paper. Whenever he sees something interesting online, his secretary prints it on beige paper. "White is not a good contrast against black words. Beige is better," he said. The important articles are laminated. "Anything that is laminated will not go bad," he explained.

While Lee Kuan Yew had a famous red box, which contained his daily work, Yeo has a far less famous green bag. Every day, his secretary packs a green reusable bag with reading materials – printed on beige paper, of course – which he takes home to read. It contains topics ranging from science to history, from economics to politics. Former EDB and A*STAR scholar Lisa Ooi called him "an oracle". Tan Chorh Chuan, who worked with Yeo on Singapore's biomedical sciences push, added: "He's an avid reader and reads at an incredible speed. He can read a whole book in one or two days. He also has highlighters in his bag, which he uses to highlight portions of the book that are significant to him. It's not as though he goes through the readings without understanding. He was able to master enough domain knowledge (on biomedical sciences matters) very very quickly. He was very, very impressive." Quite a statement coming from the president of the National University of Singapore.

As much as he likes text, Yeo's first love is cartoons and comics. He enjoyed browsing at comic stalls near Cathay cinema as a child and he remains captivated by the allure of illustrations. "Comics is the ultimate tool for communication," he said. "In one image or a few images, you convey everything." He loves the political cartoons of the *New Yorker* magazine and files them away on, yes beige paper. When he was chairman of A*STAR, its 2006/7 annual report carried cartoons of whales and guppies, which refer to top scientists and young researchers respectively. "Tell me which agency in Singapore has annual reports with cartoons?" he asked with a laugh. It helps that he has a wicked sense of humour. When he was running defence firm Chartered Industries of Singapore (CIS) in the 1980s, Yeo promised his CEO Lai Chun Loong that he would reward him with a Rolls Royce if he could make S$100 million in overseas sales contracts. Lai did it. During a business trip to Zurich, Yeo brought Lai to a toy shop and bought him a Dinky Toy Rolls Royce. "That's the Rolls Royce for you," said Yeo.

His voracious reading and quick grasp of concepts earned him good grades in SJI and a ticket out of poverty. He said: "When I did well in school, I got prizes, usually books. I got rewards which I wouldn't have been able to afford. So it was an incentive to study hard." His six enriching years at SJI made him a strong supporter of the school. When his alma mater wanted to branch into an international school in 2006, Yeo helped raise funds through his network. "The idea of a homegrown, international school resonated strongly with Philip," said Commissioner of Inland Revenue Tan Tee How, who was among the key drivers of the SJI International School project. "He also saw this as an opportunity for Josephians like himself to 'give back' to our alma mater."

But while Yeo was loquacious of almost everything in his life, from details of his first pay cheque (S$900) to even a recent bout of diarrhoea, he was tight-lipped and protective about the most constant companion of his volatile life – his wife, Jane. They got married in 1971, a year after he started work. He shared that she has always stayed in the background, looking after their family while he built his career and became an increasingly famous public figure. "Most of the time, my wife and children do not tell people who their husband and father is," he said.

After much persuasion, Jane agreed to pen her thoughts on Philip and their family. She explained why they are more comfortable out of the limelight:

"My kids and I prefer not to let others know about Philip as we observed that people's attitudes could change with that knowledge, depending on how they perceive Philip. Some of those who dislike him and his policies would regard us with contempt and prejudiced treatment, while some others who do like him may view our abilities and worth as a reflection of Philip's successes, rather than our own personal achievements.

29

"When it is discovered that we are related to Philip Yeo, oftentimes, we are no longer recognised as simply being our own persons. Instead, our thoughts, our actions and our very being become scrutinised as representations of Philip Yeo. That is why we feel that it is best to be just us and not the wife or son or daughter of Philip Yeo. In fact, we never inform the people whom we have just met, or even our work colleagues, of who he is. In order to avoid such potential complications, my children even preferred me to meet with their teachers during their school days for parent-teacher meetings.

"Yet, interestingly, many of these people eventually find out about our relationship with Philip on their own, which is when we then brace ourselves for impact – will their attitudes change or will they stay the same? Of course, not everyone responds this way – each of our close friends certainly does not, and my children and I are grateful for these friends. I am proud to say my kids are humble and work hard to carve out their own lives, rather than rely on Philip's status and reputation."

Philip Yeo opened up considerably when talking about their two children, Eugene and Elaine. Eugene, 39, is a professor at University of California, San Diego, while Elaine, 30, is a psychologist. Both are engaged. Yeo shared freely about their childhood, their stellar grades in school and their shared passion for comics – Marvel for Eugene and Japanese manga for Elaine. The wallpaper of his new iPad Pro is of Eugene ziplining and Elaine on a quad bike. At home and at work, he proudly showcases photographs highlighting his children's academic and professional achievements. "I've always felt that he was unnaturally proud of us," said Eugene. "I'm like: Why? This is what I'm supposed to be doing anyway, right?"

Philip Yeo credited his wife for taking care of the children. "When they were growing up, I was not around most of the time. When I was chairman of EDB, I travelled a lot. So my wife took care of our kids. She ensured they did their work and did well in school," he said. She did more than that. Said Jane: "Our kids had accepted that their father was often not home. I sent my children for swimming lessons, piano lessons and other activities. I also read to them when they were young. Philip bought them lots of books on his travels. My kids are fond of books and they could be kept preoccupied with books or their favourite toys from their father. Whenever Philip is home, he would spend time with the family. Hence, he usually does not have much time for socialising."

Yeo made sure he was available for his children. His secretary Mary Chan called him "a most doting father". Said Eugene: "He's sort of

30

omnipresent. When you need him, he will appear. I think that's better than a father who was always around but would disappear when you need him." He called his dad an "enabler". "He gave us a lot of freedom," said Eugene. "So he would say, 'Oh you like manga? Okay, fine, go read as much as you want.' Our library at home is full of my sister's manga books and it's thanks to that freedom that she went on to study Japanese and is now fluent in the language." Jane shared that they have never felt neglected, neither do they object to his busy schedule. "Instead, we were very supportive of him and proud of his years of achievement. He was quite recognised by the public during the EDB days," she said.

But there are clear lines drawn between the public Philip Yeo persona and the private man, said his son. He likened him to Shrek, the fictional ogre character in the eponymous movie. "In the work environment, he comes across as hard, efficient and tough," he said. "I've seen one of his uniformed people cry when he was in Mindef. But he's mushy, like marshmallow, inside. The family gets to see the inside because we're in that realm. I remember when I was like nine or 10, he once said, 'If you want to be a leader some day, one thing you will know for sure is that a leader is very lonely.' That stuck with me and I could see it in his life. People come and people go as they went on their separate ways. We are not a family where there are friends coming over every weekend. We don't have parties. When he's home, he's just with his family. He's got a larger network than most people do, but at the end, it's a very lonely network because they are mostly colleagues and work people. I don't think he has many truly close friends who have not been in some way or form tied to his work. It's just family."

He is the Lone Ranger.

Q *What do you remember of your childhood?*

A I did my own things. My mum was busy and so I ran around and was very independent. Nobody disturbed me.

Q *And you enjoyed that?*

A I enjoyed the freedom to do whatever I wanted. In school, I would finish my maths homework months in advance.

Q *Months in advance?*

A Yes, yes, I would go through three months of exercises at one go and submit them to my teacher. He loved me because I finished so fast. Then I asked to go to the library. That's the reason why I became a librarian. I didn't want to stay in class and being a librarian gave me a reason to escape. It helped that the library was the only place in SJI that was air-conditioned. So it was a nice place to relax and read. It was better than staying in class. When I was younger, I would finish my work very fast and I would get bored. The teacher didn't allow me to doodle or walk around. So when I did, I was punished and made to stand at the blackboard. I would look at spiders crawling around. I was never one of the kids who could sit still. Those obedient kids are the ones who would make good Administrative Officers. They won't be entrepreneurs.

Q *Would you consider yourself a rebel when you were young?*

A I was independent. I don't think I rebelled. I just did my own thing. To make sure I could do things, I complied with some regimental duty.

I liked to be left alone. Even later in life, that was how I approached work. I never visited my bosses during Chinese New Year or invite my staff to my place. A holiday is my holiday.

Q *Was that the case too during your days at the University of Toronto?*

A I was always independent, I didn't depend on anybody. I could always make money. Even in Canada, I worked illegally. In the first year, I did summer work in the lab with PhD students. But there was no money. In the second summer, I worked in a factory making windows. I was paid C$1.75 an hour. In that summer, I earned C$3,000 and and C$1 was equivalent to S$3 then. In my third year, I went to Vancouver to work for an industrial engineering consulting firm for a month. And every Friday, I washed dishes in a restaurant outside Toronto. With all the money made, I could come back to Singapore for a holiday.

Q *To see your girlfriend?*

A In those days, there was no e-mail. So we wrote letters.

Q *How did she cope as you rose up the civil service and during your more controversial moments?*

A Most of the time, she didn't want people to know who I was. She prefers to be private. The same goes for my kids. When my son was in Catholic High, very few people knew he was my son. When he completed his studies there as one of the top students, I went to the school for his PSLE results. The principal recognised me and that was when the school found out. Usually, I never bothered or disturbed my son in school. It was the same for my daughter. My wife attended the parent-teacher sessions for both my kids during their primary and secondary days.

Q   *Did your wife ever ask you to tone down?*

A   Only when I scolded people. She would tell me not to scold people, and not be so rude. I can't change. How can people change? We all can't change. People are people. Mrs Lee used to be able to calm Lee Kuan Yew down. She moderated him. What's the famous word? "Haaaarry". But my wife couldn't moderate me.

Q   *You got married after your graduation?*

A   I graduated in 1970 and we got married the next year. The moment I finished my last exam in Toronto, I came home. I didn't even wait for the graduation ceremony. I wanted to look for a job and start earning money.

Q   *Why did you have to look for a job when you were bonded to work in the civil service?*

A   In those days, you may have a scholarship but you had no idea what was lined up for you. I didn't even know whether there was a job. The PSC[1] never told me where I was going to be posted to and what I was supposed to do. They just said "come back". I didn't want to sit around waiting because that means I wouldn't get paid. There were some scholars who came back after me and they were jobless for three months because they were waiting to be interviewed by the PSC. PSC also didn't know what to do with me because I

---

1   PSC refers to the Public Service Commission, which is in charge of the administration of scholarships in the civil service, among its other duties.

studied industrial engineering. At that time, all the scholars studied mechanical, civil or electrical engineering.

Q *What did you manage to find?*

A I applied for a job with Litton Industries and the managing director was very keen to have me. He offered me a job to be his assistant. Litton was an American electronics company. I was very keen. I didn't want to join the government. I was trying to convince PSC to release me.

Q *So you wanted to break your bond?*

A I was hoping they would release me from my bond since they didn't know what to do with me. I was trying ways and means to run away. If I were not bonded, I'll be living in Canada. It was my first attempt to escape from the civil service. But PSC said: "Sorry, we cannot release you." So a week later, there was another advertisement to join EDB. EDB had set up the EIDA – Engineering Industry Development Agency, to train technical workers. I applied to them, they approved and wanted me to be an engineer. I was slated to go for medical examination. Again, I asked PSC and again they refused to release me.

Now, I was getting pissed off. I wanted a job and they were not giving me a job and yet they refused to let me take up other jobs. By the third week after I returned from Toronto, I went to the PSC and I complained to them: "Hey, I've got no job for three weeks. What's going on?" To shut me up, they finally gave me a posting. They sent me to the Ministry of Finance to do the government budget. They didn't bother to interview me. They just packed me off.

Q   *So were you satisfied?*

A   Well, at least I got a job and a salary. But it was not the kind of job I was interested in. I complained to the deputy secretary of the ministry: "What kind of job is this? This is not an engineering job." It was a very easy job. All the requests for Budget came in September. It must be completed by February. The minister announced the Budget in March. Once the Budget was approved, there wasn't much to do from March to September. I remember the office had lots of magazines and you spent your time reading magazines.

I was so bored. My account was Ministry of Health and their main budget request for the year 1970 was a new hospital wing for Singapore General Hospital (SGH). So I went to SGH and saw Dr Andrew Chew, the medical superintendent of SGH. And he said: "You're the first officer to come and see us." I said I wanted to see what he needed and he explained it to me. I couldn't imagine myself sitting in that department for five years of my bond. After one month, I asked for a new job. They said Mindef was looking for engineers and that's how I went to Mindef. I went there at nobody's request. I have an itchy backside.[2]

Q   *Were you happy to go to Mindef?*

A   Happy, very happy.

---

2   "Itchy backside" is a Singlish term that refers to someone who lands himself in a sticky situation of his own accord.

The transfer to Mindef set the scene for Philip Yeo's four-decade long career in the public service, paving the way for the brash young man to begin a stunning run in the Singapore government. He may not be enticed by the civil service, but the move to a masculine arena of action, warfare and weapons suited the tinkerer perfectly. It helped that he would soon meet a mentor who would change his life. The Lone Ranger was on the prowl and would soon cease to be a solo fighter.

defending
the nation

2

The Engineer of Combat

"You are a prime minister but you don't have any army."

Old Guard Goh Keng Swee to Prime Minister Lee Kuan Yew
when Singapore became independent in 1965

When Philip Yeo took on his new role as a branch head in the Logistics Division of Mindef in 1970, he quickly realised that something was amiss. Despite a daunting brief to develop logistic systems to help equip, clothe and feed a new fighting force, he was given only four staff. It was not enough. But his Systems and Research Branch had neither the resources nor the headcount for more. He decided to launch his career's first, and possibly still the most audacious, case of talent kidnapping.

He pored over computer printouts of personnel in the military, a skill he picked up in his undergraduate days, and meticulously studied thousands of unknown names of conscripts. He was looking for three things: education qualifications, field of study and physical deficiencies. He wanted only a particular profile: university graduates who studied engineering and preferably unable to march straight. "They were medically unfit. We called them 'one eye, one leg'. They couldn't march properly and they wore thick spectacles. They were not combatants. They were not infantry material," he said. "In fact, if you were combat fit, you would be stuck in the battalions. So most of them were misemployed. They were all clerks and storemen. There were so many of them. In those days we had around 25,000 conscripts enlisted and there was a lot of poor usage."

He visited every logistics camp and struck a deal with the commanding officers for these non-combatants to be transferred to him – with one condition. "They remain with you on paper but they work for me," he told them. Despite having next to nothing to gain from the deal, they agreed. "They didn't know what to do with them," recalled Yeo with a broad grin, no doubt still gleeful at the mass abductions nearly half a century later. The combat units continued to pay these soldiers' monthly salaries of S$90. For the soldiers, the move was a no-brainer. "I say, 'I offer you no guard duty, no uniform and no need to salute officers,'" said Yeo. He "nabbed" 250 of them, all of whom were engineering graduates, without paying a cent.

The influx of manpower caught many by surprise, including Defence Minister Goh Keng Swee. "How did Philip get so many people?" he asked, according to Yeo in an interview for the public service's archives. But he laughed and left the wandering young men alone. Said Yeo: "One good thing about Dr Goh is this: if you could get away with something, he would laugh – not your fault if you got away with it. If I kept somebody, he would say, 'good luck to you.'" Dr Goh even said that these people were "stolen" and referred to them as "Philip Yeo's illegals".

Yeo gave them a more respectable name. He called them "systems engineers", an appropriate term since he ran the Systems and Research Branch. "I took all engineers from different backgrounds, whether it was mechanical or civil or industrial, put them together and they solved every problem there was to solve. It's *rojak*," he said, referring to a famous local salad of mixed vegetables and fruits, often used as a metaphor for diversity. The term "systems engineers" would later enter the folklore of Singapore governance when they helped not only to computerise the nation but also to recommend and implement streaming – putting pupils into different courses based on their academic abilities – in the country's education system.

The sleight of hand with the 250 systems engineers was the start of Yeo's lifelong passion for talent scouting, a trait which he would carry with him to the EDB and later to A*STAR. The daredevil manoeuvre also introduced the young man to Mindef and to the Singapore government and vice versa. He was only 24 and it was already clear that he could deliver the goods, albeit operating on the margins of permissibility and, at times, legality. Rules, as he likes to say, are meant to be broken – if it is for the larger good. And he thrived on that challenge. Former Cabinet Minister George Yeo, who worked with him in Mindef, said Philip Yeo would not let rules stand in the way of a solution. "His instinct is to solve a problem. The rules are there to help us solve problems. No, I won't say that he broke rules," he said. "I think he was quite careful to make sure that things were properly done. But he was famously impatient with bean counters – people who get so preoccupied with rules that they forget the purpose of regulations." Such rebel instincts quickly found their comfort zone in the chaos that was the Singapore Armed Forces (SAF) in 1970.

When Singapore went it alone with Independence in 1965, it had two battalions, made up of mostly Malaysians and under the command of a Malaysian brigadier. As Goh famously told Prime Minister Lee Kuan Yew: "You are a prime minister but you don't have any army." The only protection the new nation had from its neighbours was the British military, which Lee and Goh had hoped would stay for another five to 10 years. It was, as Lee recalled in his memoirs, so as "to provide a shield behind which we could build up our own forces". There was no such luxury. In January 1968, the British announced their withdrawal, a pullout which was largely completed by 1971. Singapore had to build its armed forces quickly. *Military Technology*, an international defence journal, wrote in 1990 that the country "had virtually nothing in the way of armed forces to defend itself" in 1965. Conscription took care of the manpower. Thousands of young Singaporean men were drafted. But the SAF was not ready for the massive injection of soldiers. It didn't have enough boots, trucks and bullets to prepare and train these young men to become fighters. It didn't have much of anything. The unsexy and unenviable job of equipping them fell on the Logistics Division and Yeo.

"We had to equip the conscript soldiers – uniforms, food, weapons, trucks, tanks, everything. It was a big job," he said. "It was easy to enlist the recruits. But to equip them and to house them, trust me, it wasn't easy. It took time." He called himself a *karung guni* man, or rag and bone man, who went around the island amassing surplus equipment left behind by the withdrawing British forces. To make things worse, few in SAF had any idea what to do. While the combat operations had experienced operational consultants, the logistics side had little help. "At the Logistics Bases, we had 9,000 employees and 9,000 employees were all equally blur," said Yeo, using a local slang which means confused and ignorant. The mess and confusion suited the young civil servant perfectly. "It was chaos, which was good, because I could do whatever I liked," he said.

Well, not exactly. Despite the confusion and the freedom he was afforded, there was precious little for him to work with. Skilled labour in the SAF was sorely lacking. To train these "blur" workers, the military tapped on a massive 70,000 civilian workforce retrenched by the departing British. It would also help provide jobs at a time when unemployment remained high

43

at about 10 per cent. "They were most useful. They all came with skills," said Yeo. He was given the authority to interview, select and recruit them. Some had experience in storekeeping, cooking, vehicle repairs and machining, but a lot of them had no paper qualifications or special skills. Many of these jobless men were twice his age. "Grown men in neat lines faced us, a group of rookie Mindef officers, most of whom had no prior working experience," he recalled in an essay.

"These Malays, Chinese, and Indians anxiously awaited their interview to describe what they actually did in the British Army and hopefully, get a new job and an SAF pay packet. Most of them started by telling us about the size of their families and how they were the main wage earners. For them, staying employed was not an option; it was a necessity." This sobering experience would shape Yeo in his subsequent decades in public service, a constant reminder that job creation must be the raison d'etre of his career. As he said: "I learnt with humility that unemployment brings down even the hardest of men, that there is no better way to secure the future than to go out to create it."

Within a year, in 1971, he was promoted from branch head to department head, running the Organisation and Control Department. But it was neither organised nor in control. In fact, the department was nicknamed "out of control", he recalled with a loud chuckle. "There was no system. We are supposed to be organised, only then can you exercise control. But there was no system – no accounting system, and no proper procurement system." When he hired contractors to repair abandoned British military trucks, which the SAF desperately needed, he paid cash. "Those were desperate days. There was no time for rules. Anything to get things done," he said.

To cope, he relied on his old sleight of hand trick. When Goh made camp

44

visits, he would transfer equipment and clothing from another unit so that the one on inspection would not look bare. When commanders complained about having their things taken away, he admitted he threatened them. "If you complain, you get low priority when the new supply comes. So yes, this is blackmail," he said with a laugh. The shuffling, as he called it, was necessary because procurement took time and logistics was chaotic. "Borrow from Peter to pay Paul," he said. "The army was so desperate, everything was late, and everything was not ready. We had to find solutions."

His gung ho spirit was clearly noticed. Seah Kia Ger, a colleague in the Finance Division of Mindef, said it was obvious that Yeo would be a rising star. "There were other Colombo Plan scholars, but none of them were like Philip Yeo," he said. "He had good ideas, could implement those ideas and was always running around. I remembered thinking he was like a rat, constantly scurrying about. He stood out." Yeo's superiors shared the same assessment. By 1972, he was made Director of the Finance Division, one of five divisions in the ministry. The 26-year-old had only the Permanent Secretary and the Minister above him in Mindef's flat hierarchy. He was paid S$1,000 a month, given a Mercedes Benz as his official car – the licence plate was MID14, he remembered fondly – and a national serviceman as a driver. Those were heady days. When contractors complained of slow payment from Mindef, he requested authority to sign cheques of up to a million Singapore dollars. It was unheard of in the government. "Finance Division had to check the bills, then we sent the bills for payment to the accountant-general. They took months to process," he said. "I told Dr Goh the contractors were suffering. 'So what do you want?' he asked. I said I wanted authority to sign cheques. He said okay."

It was clear, even in those early years, that he had formed a strong

45

working relationship with Goh, whom he affectionately refers to as "old man". The minister, who died in 2010, was famously impatient, inquisitive and efficient. Yeo was a younger replica. Ko Kheng Hwa, one of Yeo's systems engineers, described him with five words: "Quick, quick, quick, fast, fast." Singapore's Chinese daily *Lianhe Zaobao*, in an article in 2015, described Yeo's relationship with Goh as "akin to Bo Le, a horse connoisseur in ancient China, taming a good horse when none could". Although the equine young Yeo was a junior civil servant, the flat administrative structure of Mindef afforded him plenty of face time with his tamer, Goh. It helped too that his superior Ong Kah Kok, Director of Logistics Division, a contemporary of Goh, was only too happy to send Yeo to answer Goh's many queries and commands. Said Yeo: "Ong would find all kinds of excuses to not meet Dr Goh. So I became his surrogate. They knew each other. So this guy, he *bo chap*[3] Dr Goh. He would ask me to go and see the old man. So I've got to do it. He was my boss."

The interaction between the seasoned politician and the young bureaucrat, separated by a 28-year age gap, took on several forms. There were the regular camp visits mentioned earlier, when Goh would travel in a military helicopter, accompanied by Yeo. The young civil servant was also at the receiving end of frequent calls to the boss' office for a quick directive. "Conversations were very short – 'I want this thing solved.' No sermon on the mount – very straightforward. So I learnt to find out what he wanted, and just said 'okay, okay', and got out to do it. I didn't hang around," he said.

More importantly, Yeo participated in the weekly Monday meetings at Mindef with the division directors and chaired by Goh. By Friday, the

---

3   *Bo chap* is Hokkien for "can't be bothered".

directors received their papers on Monday's agenda, which they would read over the weekend before meeting at 11am on Monday. The meetings were usually short and would be over by 1pm. They would break for lunch and continue the discussions afterwards. For issues without a resolution, Goh expected an answer by 5pm the same day. "That's the old man's style," Yeo said. The meetings must have curry puffs from the well-known Polar cafe. Goh was a diabetic and needed regular snacks to sustain his energy through the day. "He must have something to eat. So if he didn't get his curry puff, he would be in a bad mood, and we would all be in trouble," he said. Curry puffs remain a regular item in Yeo's office today, perhaps as a dietary tribute to his mentor. Several interviews for this book were done with a plate of the savoury and spicy pastries in the middle of the table. Similarly, Yeo would emulate Goh's decisiveness and short meetings. "When it comes to meetings, Philip Yeo already made up his mind whether to go ahead or not," said Goh Song How, who started working with Yeo in Mindef. "We would have a very quick presentation and skip a lot of points because he would say, 'I've read it before. Here's the budget and the deadline. Go do it.'"

Work did not end in the evening. Yeo had to accompany Goh on frequent working dinners because Ong didn't want to be involved. These dinners were usually with foreign dignitaries and local businessmen and stretched late into the night. "I was home for only one or two nights a week," said Yeo. "Those were the days of a six-day work week and with Dr Goh, every day was a working day. Work-life balance? You've got to be kidding." His wife, Jane, added: "He would leave early for office and return home late. He worked very hard and quietly I supported him without any objections or feelings of neglect." Those dinners gave him valuable contacts with not only foreign military leaders, but also local tycoons. He would tap these important people for support later in his career.

The bond between Goh and Yeo, forged in the early chaotic years of the SAF, would continue to strengthen over the next decades. Yeo would mention Goh in every single interview for this book, as well as in almost every one of his important speeches during his public service career. He attributes most of his success to the tutelage of the late leader. Veteran EDB alumnus Khoo Seok Lin said that she had seen Yeo nervous only once, prior to a presentation to Goh in the late 1980s. "He told me to do the presentation and he wanted to go through the slides. That's something he never did. Usually, he would just let you do whatever you wanted. But at that time, he was nervous. He reminded me not to speak too fast because Dr Goh wouldn't be able to hear. Talk about pot calling the kettle black!" Another EDB old hand and former politician David Lim went so far as to say: "Dr Goh was like a mini god to Philip."

The relationship became a central theme of Yeo's career narrative through public service, a rare connection between a politician and a bureaucrat. In fact, Yeo would say repeatedly, only half in jest, that he "blames" Dr Goh for keeping him in the civil service. Otherwise, he would have left for the private sector. The master-disciple ties would also have a larger impact on Singapore, stretching far beyond the military and into the economy, education, transport and technology.

48

Q   *There is an urban legend in the SAF of how you threw someone's table out of his office because you wanted it. Is it true?*

A   It is true. I asked him nicely if he could move and he refused to. I asked: "Can you please move? I have no place." I had all these "illegals" (the 250 systems engineers) coming in. He kept quiet. So I called my National Service boys, took his senior officer's desk, his chair and his cabinet and put them in the corridor. His name was Basil Fox, a Group Captain[4] with the British air force. He was seconded to the SAF. He was head of Air Logistics and he was supposed to move to another building in Mindef and I was supposed to take over this office.

Q   *How did he react?*

A   Oh, he was very upset. He complained straightaway to Sir Rochford Hughes, who was the air adviser to Dr Goh, to Mindef Permanent Secretary Pang Tee Pow and Dr Goh. They all had a good laugh. If I didn't move the table and chair, he would not. Basically, it would be nice for him to move. I knew he wouldn't move. But we became good friends and when I became chairman of Chartered Industries of Singapore (CIS) and Unicorn International, I recruited Basil to help me until he passed away. I took care of Basil and his wife when they stayed in Singapore. They never went back home. He had stayed in Singapore all the time – a very good and loyal guy.

Q   *Dr Goh seemed to back you in almost everything you did. How did you gain his trust?*

A   Just do your job, whatever the job. Every time he had a job, he would call me: "I need this done." And I would send a team to get it done

---

4   Group captain is equivalent to the colonel rank in the army.

Once, he called me up and said he wanted to build squash courts for the army. He said he wanted to equip every battalion with a squash court. I said yes.

Q *Why squash courts?*

A We wanted the officers to be fit.

Q *But why squash?*

A Squash is a very fast game.

Q *Why not badminton?*

A A squash court is very small and it is indoors – saves space. So he said we needed S$10 million and we would not use the defence budget. So what are you planning to do, I asked. He said we should try to raise money from donors. There was no money from Finance. He didn't want to ask the government for money. So I said: "Dr Goh, okay, we arrange dinner, right?" I learnt to be a professional beggar because I knew who to invite as guests after going to all the dinners I accompanied Dr Goh to. So I invited all the guests – old friends, Lien Ying Chow, Wee Cho Yaw ...[5] they all coughed up S$10 million in one meal. Not bad. That's how I learnt to hustle for money. And old man was very good. He never said anything about money. He just said we needed it and then I would follow up.

Q *That's a lot of money at that time?*

A Yes, a lot of money. So every battalion had squash courts. Then he

5   Lien Ying Chow was a founder of the defunct Overseas Union Bank.
     Wee Cho Yaw is the chairman of the United Overseas Bank.

said he wanted the officers to play polo. Wow, big problem. Winston Choo, the Chief of General Staff, had to get horses. Old man was the smartest minister. He wanted officers to be very fit. But my god, where to get the horses? Got to buy, right? So we talked to the Polo Club. And we came back and told the old man that it's a very expensive hobby. It didn't take off.

Q   *Why polo?*

A   He always believed in cavalry. British army officers all played polo. It's a skill, you know. They used a ball or a goat's head. In the old days, they used the enemy's head. You know, you on the horse, it's like fighting, combating. So polo trains the officers. Dr Goh had this idea that the officer cadet should be like the German general staff – something unique. So the squash court was only for officers. At one time he wanted all SAF officers to learn to play bridge. Intellectual, right? The old man played bridge. I don't play bridge. It's a waste of my time. After a while the bridge experiment died too. He was quite a unique character. We were all terrified of him because he just stared at you with his beady eyes. He didn't scold.

Q   *Can you recall an instance when he was very angry and how you coped with it?*

A   In 1971, I was head of "out of control", remember? One day, Pang Tee Pow came into the office and said that Dr Goh wanted to shut down the SAF Technical Training Institute (SAFTECH). All the army technicians and machinists were trained in SAFTECH in Seletar Air Base. Dr Goh went to visit the camp. I was not with him on that trip. When he came back, he was very angry. There were a lot of complaints from the army units that the institute was out of touch and too theoretical. He told Pang that he wanted it closed down. Pang told Ong Kah Kok to do it. Ong called me, "Can you please go and see the old man?" That was on a Friday.

So I went home, sat down and looked at the organisation structure of SAFTECH. There were the weapons technicians, the automotive technicians, the optics technicians, all the different vocations. And since SAF had many bases, I took them out group by group according to vocations and transferred them to the various bases such as ammo, vehicle, ordnance. By Sunday, I drew up all the transfers. By Monday, I gave the posting orders. On the same day, I reported to Dr Goh, "All done." I saved the institute. I transferred them … different components, different places. So by Monday, there was no SAFTECH, the biggest technical school in Mindef. It disappeared. No fuss. All the men were transferred. Except for the commanding officer, nobody lost their jobs. They were just moved to another place. I was only in my mid-20s and I had to save people's lives. This happened in other instances too. Pang Tee Pow would chop[6] someone based on Dr Goh's instructions. Then he would call me: "Philip, can you take care of this?" So I had to find the guy a job. I learnt to take care of people in a quiet way without those people knowing.

So in that sense, Dr Goh can be very tough. He won't have the patience to listen to your sob stories, no. But for me, I learnt how to handle the old man. Get the job done. Don't go into too much details and he would leave me alone. That was how I trained my EDB officers too. Why do I want them to tell me their *lor sor*[7] stories? If that's the case, I might as well do it myself. And that's a very important trait I learnt from old man. He asked you to do, get it done. Don't tell him too much. Then you have freedom to do it. If you ask for step one to three, you are going to get into trouble. I also learnt from him not to

---

6   To "chop" is to remove someone from his job in Singlish.
7   *Lor sor* is Cantonese for "long-winded".

try to rebuild. Burn it down, restart. He believed in what's called the "phoenix theory". The old man taught me: you try to change ... it's very hard to change. So, always restart, then you will not be bounded by legacies. And he's quite right. That's the way it was working with Dr Goh. Very dangerous living!

Q   *What are the other examples of him burning it down?*

A   After he became deputy prime minister in 1973, he wanted to destroy all the pig farms because they were polluting. One day, he called me in and said: "I'm now in charge of PPD.[8] The pig farms are polluting. Can you get an old tanker, create layers, move all the pigs into the tanker, sail into the South China Sea? Let the pigs pollute the sea." I said okay, I would study it. But tankers are hot, and pigs would die of heat stroke. So I went back to Dr Goh and told him that we can't pack all the pigs into a tanker. The idea was dropped. Years later, I visited Pulau Bulan, from where we imported 400,000 pigs per year. Every day, 1 per cent or so die from heat stroke. Why are pigs dirty? They are not dirty. They are trying to keep themselves cool. The pigs need to roll in mud and water to keep cool. Otherwise, they will overheat.

Q   *Pig farms are completely unrelated to Mindef work. Why were you tasked to look into it?*

A   That's how Dr Goh worked. He had a hand in almost everything. And we worked for the boss – old man Dr Goh. I called some of what he asked us to do "mission impossible", like the pigs experiment. But whatever he told us to do, we did it. What's the big deal, right? You must understand engineers' minds. Engineers believe they can solve

---

8   PPD refers to the Primary Production Department, the predecessor of the Agri-Food and Veterinary Authority.

anything. It's a matter of time and how you do it. It's a mentality. We don't argue about the philosophical or moral value. Put the pig on a tanker, the poor pig will die – overheat, right? That's it. We're basically problem solvers.

Q   *You didn't find it troublesome that this took you away from what you were doing?*

A   I just did extra work. My day-to-day work was logistics, solving all the problems. It was good that I had a lot of NS (National Service) officers who were graduates, who were mis-employed. So I used them as systems engineers. And they were happy because I gave them real work – no uniform, no guard duty, no need to salute anyone – when you are an NSF (Full-time National Serviceman), you have to salute people every day. The systems engineers were divided into three categories: the NSFs, the civil servants in Mindef and also scholars like David Lim, Tan Chin Nam, Ko Kheng Hwa and Lim Swee Say.[9]

Q   *Despite doing all this work, you were getting restless in Mindef?*

A   I got the authority to sign cheques, I processed all the payments and I got the accounting system in place, everything had been done. Dr Goh called me up in mid-1973 and said: "You're bored." I said: "Ya, I have finished my work. All done." So he asked me: "Can you take a look at the bus system?" The buses were in a mess. All the bus companies were losing money; there were overcrowding, duplication of routes, buses breaking down. So I set up a team of systems engineers and we went all over Singapore looking at buses of Hock Lee, Tay Koh Yat, STC (Singapore Traction Company) and so on. I came back with the recommendation to merge the companies into one organisation

---

9   Lim Swee Say and David Lim became Cabinet ministers. Tan Chin Nam rose to the ranks of permanent secretary. Ko Kheng Hwa took on various senior positions in the public sector including CEO of JTC Corporation and EDB.

– the Singapore Bus Services (SBS). Dr Goh wrote to Prime Minister Lee Kuan Yew and it was approved. He came back to me and said: "So Philip, we appoint you as general manager of SBS." But I told him: "Erm, Dr Goh, I'm going to Harvard, you know?" I had applied to do an MBA at Harvard.

Q *Why did you want to leave for Harvard at that point?*

A While working with the old man, I was alone every night. I wanted to get out. In those days, we signed a five-year bond for our PSC scholarship. By August 1974, I had finished four years. Once my bond was up, I *zao*.[10] I have never considered myself a civil servant. I was there because I had a bond to honour. I wanted to do my MBA and I applied for the Fulbright scholarship. It was paid by the US State Department. Not the PSC. But PSC did the selection and it carried a second five-year bond with the Singapore government.

Q *There was a five-year bond even though it was not paid by the government?*

A I thought Fulbright was good but I didn't realise that there was a bond. Actually it wasn't fair. At the end of the day, I got into another bond. Argh ...

Q *Why didn't you want to stay?*

A I never imagined I would be a civil servant. I never planned to be one. I took a scholarship to study. That was all I wanted. If not for Dr Goh's intervention, I would have left. I wanted to go into the industry – I'd probably be richer now. So let me give you an example. In 1974,

---

10 *Zao* is Hokkien for "run away".

I was into my fourth year in the Administrative Service. But my boss Pang Tee Pow realised that I was still not confirmed. At that time, you had to take the Instruction Manuals 1, 2 and 3 and Standard One Mandarin exams to be confirmed and promoted. I didn't do it so they didn't confirm me. My contemporaries took all the exams and were promoted to Senior Engineers. I was still Administrative Assistant (AA), the lowest grade. So I thought to myself: "I don't care. If I'm not confirmed, then I don't have to stay."

Pang went to tell Dr Goh that I was not confirmed and I was not promoted. I didn't complain. Dr Goh went to ask Mr Tan Teck Chwee, chairman of PSC, and scolded him over the phone. Tan was very angry, called me up for lunch. I said: "Mr Tan, I did not do anything. I don't know what happened." He called me a troublemaker. He advised: "You should quit the government and join me." He owned a construction company. So I told him: "If I quit and join you, two of us will be in trouble with Dr Goh." But Tan realised it was not my fault.

Q *So after that lunch, you were finally confirmed?*

A Yes. I left in August 1974 to go to Harvard Business School. Within weeks, I received a PSC letter that I was promoted. It was a double promotion from AA to Principal Assistant Secretary.

Yeo's escape plan from the civil service – his second thus far – never got close to taking off. Accompanied by his wife, he reached Harvard in 1974 and was finally able to spend some quality time with her. She said: "When we were there, I helped him to type his case studies. Some students had to pay others for typing their case studies. I used an old fashioned typewriter with carbon paper for copies." But within months after reaching Harvard in 1974, Goh sent him word to abandon studies and return home. He declined. But the memos from Singapore did not abate. The growing likelihood of US-backed South Vietnam falling to the communist North Vietnam was sending jitters through Southeast Asia. The domino theory of the Cold War cultivated a fear through the region that Saigon would be the first of many to fall into the red orbit of the communists. As former US president Richard Nixon said in 1953: "If Indochina falls, Thailand is put in an almost impossible position. The same is true of Malaya with its rubber and tin. The same is true of Indonesia."

57

On April 30, 1975, the worst fears of Asean were realised. The Vietnam War came to an end with Saigon captured by the north Vietnamese. The Americans made a humiliating retreat. The fledgling SAF had to be prepared for a possible red tide engulfing the region. Said Yeo: "Singapore was very worried. Dr Goh was very worried. Thailand would be next and then Malaysia and us. So in 1975, I was asked again by Pang Tee Pow to come back. I said no, I wanted to finish my two-year course." Pang acquiesced, but with one condition. In a letter to Yeo on January 14, 1976, he wrote: "Minister has asked when you will be finishing your course and I told him you will be coming back some time in June. He has directed that you should come back immediately after the course as your services are urgently required in Mindef." Yeo obeyed: "So that's why I came back immediately after I finished my exams. I packed up, I came home. I didn't attend the Harvard graduation. I had wanted to travel Europe with my wife before returning home. I didn't get a chance to do it."

Bullet the Blue Sky

"My chief gunrunner."

*Goh Keng Swee referring to Philip Yeo, in an undated quote,
taken from* Towards Tomorrow: The Singapore Technologies Group Story

At 2am on June 23, 1980, under the cover of darkness, some 200 Vietnamese soldiers crept across the Cambodia-Thailand border. The battle-hardened infantry, fresh from its victory over the Americans five years earlier and invasion of Cambodia, quickly occupied two Thai villages and two refugees camps housing Cambodians. One of the world's most ferocious fighting forces had opened yet another chapter in the Southeast Asia theatre of the Cold War. But victory would be elusive this round, partly thanks to a diminutive bespectacled man from Singapore.

The Thais responded with tremendous fire. They sent in F-5 jets, helicopter gunships and tanks. Close combat with small arms led to casualties on both sides, while the Thai artillery punished the Vietnamese positions. After more than 24 hours, the invaders withdrew back into Cambodia. It was a successful repulsion of the first Vietnamese incursion into a non-communist country, confirming fears across Asean, but especially in Bangkok and Singapore, that Hanoi was intent on realising the domino theory. Philip Yeo heard the news and could afford a smile. His work over the last four years had reaped some results.

Almost as soon as he returned home from Harvard in mid-1976, he was thrust into the bloody tangles of Cold War politics. Deputy Prime Minister and Defence Minister Goh Keng Swee appointed him Director of Logistics Division in Mindef. At their first meeting in two years, Goh took out a bundle of documents and handed it to his protégé, saying: "Kept these files for you for the past two years!" There was no chance for Yeo, still only 29 years old, to gradually shake off the laggardness of studies for the intensity of military and realpolitik. Goh sent him to Bangkok almost immediately. His brief was to help upgrade the armament production capability and capacity of the Thai military.

Yeo met General Kriangsak Chomanan, the supreme commander of the Thai armed forces, in late 1976, 10 months before the leader launched a coup and made himself prime minister. The young Singaporean was given full access to Thailand's defence industries, including ammunition, rifle and artillery plants. He was shocked at what he saw. "They've got ammunition stockpile for only one week," he recalled. "The Thais' logistics were not in a good shape." The *Economist* magazine famously noted in 2004, in an obituary for Kriangsak: "In General Kriangsak's time the army had 700 generals or, as one observer noted, one for every tank." The Thais were awfully candid about the abysmal state of its armoury, shared Lai Chun Loong, a long-time aide of Yeo in the defence industries. When Yeo asked them how old the machines were in a factory, the Thai general replied: "Older than you." Yeo told Goh that the Thai army would not have enough ammunition to fight a long war. Goh replied that Yeo's job was to ensure they would.

Thailand quickly became Yeo's second home. He made frequent trips up north and took 1,000 Thai technicians to Singapore, training them in

59

the latest technology in arms manufacturing. They were taught to produce mortar bombs, 500-pound aerial bombs and increase capacity for higher rifle and bullet productions. For instance, the Thais ditched the American mortar bombs they had for the longer-range Tampella Finnish model adopted by the SAF. Despite a clear incompatibility between Yeo and the Thai military leaders in language and walking pace, trust was forged. Said Lai: "Philip talked very fast and the Thais couldn't understand him sometimes. Philip walked very fast and the Thais couldn't catch up." While Singapore stopped short of supplying arms to the Thais, it provided components of weapons to speed up the Thais' armament reinforcements. "Whatever Singapore could do to help, we did," said Yeo. "Dr Goh's instruction was very clear – help the Thais."

Yeo went overtime in his assistance. Once, in the early 1980s, the Thais asked him to supply 10 million rounds of 5.56mm cartridges for the M-16 assault rifles. They had inked a contract with the Koreans but there was still no delivery after six months. Bangkok was panicking. Yeo told the Thais: "I will supply the 10 million rounds in 10 days." He asked then-Defence Minister Howe Yoon Chong for permission to borrow from Mindef to sell to Thailand, while Singapore manufactured new ones to replenish its stock. Howe joked that it was not a bad deal: "Sell old bullets while we make new bullets." Yeo recalled the challenge with relish, jabbing in the air as he said: "So, on the first night, I got our SAF army ammo base in Bukit Timah to pack one million rounds. We delivered it on a C-130 cargo aircraft to the Don Muang Airport in Bangkok. The Thais were shocked. 'Okay, one million rounds', I said, 'This is General Prem's request.'" Yeo recounted, referring to then-Thai Defence Minister General Prem Tinsulanonda.

Yeo continued: "Our ammo store-men packed the other nine million rounds and loaded them onto a Landing Ship Tank (LST) and our Singapore navy delivered them in seven days. Hey, ships travel slower. I was ahead of my 10 days. It took the Thai defence ministry one year to pay me! General Prem brought me Thai durians when we met for a private dinner in the Thai embassy in Singapore. Our agreement had no contract, no purchase order, nothing. I delivered 10 million rounds to him in seven days." Meanwhile, Chartered Industries of Singapore (CIS) produced two million rounds a month and in five months, Mindef's stock was replenished. Or as Howe said, new bullets for old bullets. Such support helped the Thais fend off the Vietnamese, ending the communist dominoes at the Thai-Cambodian border. Said Yeo: "Wars are won by logistics."

The Indo-China conflict was a brutal re-entry for Yeo into the Singapore civil service after his Harvard hiatus. While it may seem ironic, or even outlandish, for the struggling young SAF to help equip a bigger country like Thailand, the Singapore leaders clearly believed that prevention was better than cure. The same applied to the SAF. It had to build up not only troop numbers but also weapons sophistication. "One of the first things the old man said to me when I came back was that we had to build up defence capability. We had to stockpile. My idea of a stockpile was to fight for a long time," said Yeo. The setback suffered by the Israelis – Singapore's military advisers – in the 1973 war against the Arab states also added to the fear factor in the Cabinet, especially for Goh, of the vulnerability of small states.

But Goh was not content with simply purchasing weapons overseas, as was common of developing countries' military. "It's easy to buy. In fact, most countries around here do it because every time you buy something, you get a commission. Purchasing of weapons is a sought-after job in armed forces because it allows rampant corruption," said Yeo. Goh insisted on self-sufficiency and a local defence industry with export ambitions. But he also did not want the weapons to be in the hands of the military, so as to prevent coups as seen in Indonesia and Thailand. He wanted civilians to be in charge. So instead of parking the defence industry in Mindef, he created companies. The first was the CIS in 1967 to manufacture small arms ammunition and mortar bombs for the SAF. It produced the bullets which were sold to Thailand. Thereafter, more firms like Ordnance Development and Engineering (ODE), Singapore Automotive Engineering (SAE), Allied Ordnance of Singapore (AOS), Singapore Shipbuilding and Engineering (SSE) and Singapore Aerospace Maintenance Company (Samco) were launched, creating an alphabet soup of 100 per cent state-owned companies which eventually became the Singapore Technologies (ST) group.

Then-Deputy Prime Minister Lee Hsien Loong said at the 25th anniversary of CIS in 1992: "One crucial decision was to set up CIS as an independent corporate entity... the easier path would have been to do it in-house, and establish an ammunition arsenal or ordnance foundry with Mindef. This would have been less risky, at least from the point of view of CIS. As a non-commercial operation, the arsenal would have been shielded from competition, operated on a cost plus basis, and had no problems filling its order books with SAF business. Instead, CIS became a company run on commercial principles."

Yeo had been placed in charge of four of these companies, including CIS by 1979. That same year, he was made second permanent secretary of Mindef. It began a long period of his career when he took on secondary appointments, or in his words, "extra work", in addition to his day job. "In those days, I had many jobs. But only one pay," he said with a chuckle. "That was how it was with Dr Goh. If you were good, he gave you more work. But no extra pay." The extra work even ventured out of defence. In 1981, he was made the founding chairman of the National Computer Board and oversaw the computerisation of the civil service.

He was efficient, said his staff. "He would call you up directly, run through your paper and make a decision. He was very quick," said former Cabinet Minister George Yeo, who worked with Philip Yeo when he was a young officer in Mindef. "You put up a submission to him, you get a clear answer. You didn't often get asked to do further studies and therefore I liked working for him. There was a decisive quality about him." He also delegated confidently. Said Lai, who rose to be president of CIS: "He left most of the day-to-day operations to the full-time employees. He had so many other jobs on his plate. His meetings were always very short and he didn't beat around the bush. Just went straight to the point and decisions were made."

The defence industries gave Yeo useful training in business, a foundation which he would build on to much success in later years. While the firms were state-owned, they maintained an arm's length relationship with Mindef. They had to turn a profit, enjoyed no government subsidies and faced stringent external audits. Their bids for Mindef work also required them to compete openly with foreign defence suppliers. Venturing overseas further opened them to global competition. Critically, Goh decided at the outset that these war-faring companies should also benefit during peacetime. One of the departments of the CIS, for instance, was the Singapore Mint. The government realised very early on that making bullets and coins both

63

required precision engineering and high security. Thus, the defence firms, mostly led by Yeo, started branching out into a bewildering array of civilian businesses, from commercial vehicle testing to even selling roast ducks!

Instead of the proverbial bullets or butter struggle between defence or civilian spending, Singapore decided that it wanted both. It would spend on military needs and make money from civilian jobs. And in Philip Yeo, it found perhaps the most suitable person to straddle this divide – a business-minded civil servant with a strong appetite for risks and little patience for rules. Said Manpower Minister Lim Swee Say, who was one of Yeo's systems engineers in Mindef: "My first impression of Philip Yeo is that he breaks rules. He goes around corners to get things done, to make the changes he needs." Soon after Yeo's return from Harvard, he showed the SAF that attack is the best form of defence.

There were two memorable incidents. First, besides his Mindef job, Yeo was also made chairman of SAE, a company set up to provide the SAF with vehicle maintenance and servicing. The firm, which is now known as ST Kinetics, was based in an ex-British Army vehicle workshop along Ayer Rajah Road. On his first visit to the premises in June 1976, he noticed that it was packed with some 300 broken down Isuzu buses from the SBS – the consolidated bus company he had recommended to be set up before he left for Harvard.

He asked his general manager: "How long have these SBS buses been here?"

The GM responded: "Oh, they have been here for two years."

"Why are they still here?"

"Well, because SBS can't get spare parts. SBS sent them to us for repair as they can't repair them."

"Are you going to get spare parts?"

"No. We could not. SBS always complained about us."

"If you cannot repair the buses, why are you letting these broken down buses occupy our factory space?" asked Yeo.

"I don't know what to do with them."

"Call SBS."

SAE made the call and asked the bus firm to take the buses back. There was no reply. "SBS parked 300 unusable buses in SAE without charge. If they leave a bus with you for two years, do you think they need it?" he said in an interview for *Pioneers Once More*, a book on the public service in Singapore. He instructed the general manager to push all the buses out of the base. "Portsdown Road was full of broken down SBS buses. The police came. They can't blame SAE. What did SBS do? Took them back and scrapped all the buses." The Ministry of Communications, which was in charge of transport, cried foul. But Goh laughed it off. Said Yeo: "I just did it ... you think civil servants today will do that?"

Second, and the scene was again at SAE. Despite getting rid of the buses, the company was still struggling for factory space. It needed to overhaul SAF's AMX-13 tanks which were in a bad shape. Newly purchased AMX13s from the Swiss were also arriving. He spied two adjacent football fields which belonged to the SAF. During a lunch with Goh, he told the minister: "Look at the football fields. They are not being used. I need space for SAE. I'm going to take one for SAE's expansion." Goh didn't reply. Yeo wasn't waiting for one. Right after lunch, he called his hapless general manager and ordered: "Take concertina wire and fence off one football field next to SAE immediately."

By 5pm, the Singapore military had lost its first territory since the country's independence. When SAF Chief of General Staff Winston Choo complained, Goh laughed it off, again. He said: "Philip Yeo is like that." A gleeful Yeo recalled: "Dr Goh laughed but he knew what I was doing. I never paid for that land."

It was a match made in military heaven. Goh was the thinker and commander of the SAF. Yeo was his faithful tinkerer lieutenant who executed his orders unerringly. "The man who was always thinking and worrying about the defence of Singapore and global geopolitics was Dr Goh," said Yeo. "My job was to get the things done. There were no philosophical arguments. That generation didn't waste time arguing what was right and what was wrong. We just did it. The next generation would ask right or wrong, pros and cons, on the one hand and on the other hand. It's a world of difference. We were doers. We made things happen. To Dr Goh, he himself was the commander. If there were a war tomorrow, he and a handful of us civil servants would make up the command centre. That's it."

Even when Goh left for the education ministry in 1979, the relationship did not end. He wanted to bring Yeo with him but the incoming defence minister Howe pleaded for the young officer to stay. A compromise was struck. Yeo would stay in Mindef but report to Goh, who was also deputy prime minister. Howe, who oversaw the building of Toa Payoh new town and the Changi Airport as a senior civil servant, was pleased with the arrangement because he lacked the domain knowledge in defence technology affairs. Said Yeo: "Howe Yoon Chong would jokingly ask me, 'Have you seen your boss today?', meaning Dr Goh. They were good friends and Howe was a very confident minister who had no problem with me."

Yeo was given the space to pursue the triple jobs of weapons acquisition, arms development and growing the civilian businesses of the defence industry companies. It was arguably the period of his career which was most closely aligned with his personal interests. Here was a passionate engineer whose job was to purchase and create weapons amid a tense period of the Cold War. It was a practical test against life and death which he thrived on. "I'm not a theoretician. I like to take things apart physically," he said. "Give me a machine gun and the first thing I want to do is strip it. As an engineer, I want to know what goes inside these things. But please don't ask me to shoot people. I can't do that."

67

Q   *The AMX-13 tanks which Singapore bought made a big impression when they first appeared in the 1969 National Day Parade. How were they acquired?*

A   We bought those tanks from Israel. But by the time I came back from Harvard in 1976, they were breaking down and in a bad shape. We had no spare parts to repair the tanks. Fortunately, the Swiss were phasing out their AMX-13 and so they agreed to sell 151 tanks. I wanted 150 plus one extra tank so that I could strip it apart and find out how to make the tanks.

The Swiss tanks were in perfect condition because they had never gone to war. They were pristine. The earlier ones we had from the Israelis were poorly maintained because they were used in the desert. And the Swiss were very smart. When they bought the tanks, they bought spare parts to last 15 years. And all the parts were also in perfect condition. I paid only 30,000 Swiss francs per tank. Very cheap. After I negotiated with the Swiss army to buy their tanks over dinner, the Swiss colonel said, "Mr Yeo, thank you for buying our tanks. But we have also got a lot of spare parts. So you only want our tanks?"

"Yes, I've got enough spare parts," I said. It was bullshit. I needed spare parts badly. When you buy a weapon, the problem is not the weapon but the spare parts.

"But what do we do with the spare parts after we sell the tanks to you?"

"Okay, I will buy the spare parts from you."

"How do we sell it to you?"

"Go to your computer and print out the list of spare parts."

My god. The spare parts were bought in the 1950s. So I told him I would pay him 20 per cent the price he paid for them in the 1950s.

The Swiss guy was very honest. He said okay. Dr Goh said I cheated the Swiss. When the spare parts came, they were still nicely wrapped.

That was how I built up the SAF's tanks. From there, we developed our own tanks. Later, it morphed into the AMX-13 SM1 light tanks which were more reliable, mobile and faster than the original model. As much as possible, Dr Goh wanted us to produce as much as we could locally, just like the Israelis. He wanted the SAF to be self-sufficient and eventually even make enough for export. When you make something, you can repair it, change it, modify it. You are in control.

Q *As a new military, how did you manage to produce your own weapons?*

A Our defence industry had no experience. We hadn't fought a war and we had never produced anything. So everything that we did, we reverse engineered it. So when we bought the mortar bombs from overseas, for example, we just reversed engineered it. I remember briefing Mr Lee Kuan Yew, when he was prime minister, on the weapons we were producing.

"So these are the things that I'm making," I said.

"How do you do that?" he asked.

"Reverse engineer."

"What do you mean reverse engineer?"

"Copy."

Of course he wondered how the hell we did it. We were engineers. We cut the things up, measured and tried to replicate through trial and error. It was difficult. So most civil servants said, look, why do you want to do this type of thing? You just buy. Buying is easy. I just travel around the world shopping. I did that for aircraft because we didn't make aircraft. In fact, when I bought weapons, my army officers were very happy because they could go on a trip. But when I made weapons at home, the officers could only visit Jurong.

Q *What were some problems you faced in production?*

A I had a very supportive boss in Dr Goh. He told the army to be patient. He said we were all a bunch of civilians, all willing to do technical work and it would take time. We even managed to produce a GPMG (general purpose machine gun), the machine gun. The licence for it was 14 million Belgium francs and I refused to pay. So I reverse engineered it and put together a machine gun which I asked Colonel Peter Law to shoot 10,000 rounds non-stop. Then we went into full production.

Of course, you can always count on the army to *kao pei kao bu*[11] if the quality wasn't up to scratch. In most countries, the military officer procures the weapon and puts it to use on the field. In Singapore, a civilian provides the soldier with the weapon. So this separation of duties was a good way to ensure the quality of your weapons would be maintained. The army always complained: "This crazy Philip Yeo, why must he develop his own machine gun instead of buying one?" Every little thing, they *kao pei kao bu*. So we had to repair it and made sure we got it right. For the soldiers, it is one thing for the design to be right, but it is also critical that it works on the field. It must not break, crack or malfunction.

Q *Did you get into legal problems with the copying of these weapons?*

A Once, I was sued by a company. Under the licence, I could only produce for Singapore. But I was exporting it. He hired seven

---

11 *Kao pei kao bu* is a Hokkien phrase which means to "kick up a fuss".

lawyers to sue *us*. I flew to London and told him "Sir, you are suing the government. You will never win." Actually I was wrong. Legally he was right. But I managed to convince him and I offered him a one-time compensation, acknowledging it was his copyright. CIS paid a million US dollars.

Q   *Besides purchasing, copying and modifying, did Singapore's defence industry create weapons from scratch?*

A   We created the Ultimax 100, a light machine gun which is also known as a SAW (Section Automatic Weapon) in 1977. I wanted a machine gun with sustained firepower, yet light and portable. There were no such guns available on the market at that time. We bought the licence to produce M-16 rifles and we reverse engineered the GPMG. But we couldn't find anything in between. So I hired two American designers and paid them a million dollars to come up with a design. My condition was that it must be a 5.56. The normal machine gun for an individual is 7.62, a heavy, European size. So I wanted 5.56, just like the M-16.

Q   *What are 7.62 and 5.56?*

A   Bullets. Were you in the army? Oh, you're not Singaporean?

Q   *Yes, I am Singaporean.*

A   You didn't see 7.62 bullets? Your machine gun used 7.62 bullets. The bullet of your GPMG was the 7.62.

Q   *Oh, you're referring to the calibre?*

A   Ya lah. To be fair, I never shot, I just made them. I have no patience. Dr Goh would shoot. So I had to learn all this by heart and know all my ammunition. When I was permanent secretary in Mindef, I knew every bullet, every rifle, every weight.

So I wanted this gun. We had the M-16, which had only 30 round-magazines and could only shoot in bursts. Then we had the automatic GPMG, which was belt-fed but it was heavy. It weighed 11-13 kg on bipod (depending on version). I wanted something that was portable. I liked the idea of the Thompson submachine gun. So these two Americans came and designed the Ultimax with 100 rounds. It was still too heavy. We reduced it to 60 rounds. You see, in a war, most ranges are short distances. So what you want is a weapon that's able to fire continuously, kind of like burst, burst, burst. So what you want is a magazine of maximum storage. Most rifles have 30-round magazines whereas our Ultimax has 60-round magazines.

The two designers fabricated a wooden and metal mock-up and I showed it to Dr Goh. "Okay, good," he said. And we started production. If you can convince Dr Goh you have a good idea, he would give it a try. Once he thinks it is a good idea, he supports you all the way. That is quite something! Now, you would have to put up a proposal and slowly go up the hierarchy. By the time the approval is given, years would have gone by. For the Ultimax, we were able to convince him it could be done and that was it. Today it is a standard weapon in the army and we have also managed to export it.

Q   *Of all these weapons, which one are you most proud of?*

A   It's the FH-88, or Field Howitzer 88, artillery which we made. We named it after the year, 1988, when it was made operational in the SAF. It was the best 155mm calibre gun available. It was the best in range, accuracy and combat portability. Nobody in this region built a Howitzer of this capability. We put an engine into it so that we could drive the artillery gun away. When you shoot at the enemy, he could usually detect you via radar and want to *hantam*[12] you back. The trick is to shoot and then move. So a self-propelled artillery is useful, but it comes with a shorter range. Our gun had a range of 40km. If we fired it from the grounds of ODE in Jurong, we could hit the runways of Changi Airport easily. In a normal artillery detachment, there are six to nine men because of the heavy load ammunition. But with our 155mm gun, which used a hydraulic carrier, we required only three men. I placed a lot of emphasis on automation to lighten our reliance on manpower. Thanks to the good relations we had with the Thais, we tested the gun in Lopburi. I couldn't shoot in Singapore, could I?

Q *You made weapons under the defence companies like CIS and you then sell them to Mindef where you were the permanent secretary. Wasn't there a conflict of interest? Was this a normal practice in other countries?*

A In most other countries, everything is placed under the military. But for us, there are two separations. First, in Mindef, the storage of arms, ammunitions, tanks and weapons is under civilian control. Why? No coup. Dr Goh also wanted to save the soldiers for the real combat role. So the Chief of Defence Winston Choo had no control of weapons. He was only responsible for training troops. The release of the weapons must come from the defence minister and the permanent secretary, who are civilians.

Second, the production and procurement of weapons are also separated. For the defence companies, Dr Goh wanted to run them in commercial terms. When I was running the companies, I had to

---

12   *Hantam* is Malay for "pummel".

deal with Mindef as a customer. So Mindef is both customer and owner of the companies. When we first started, the companies served only Mindef. But over time, we exported the arms. When I supplied ammunition to Mindef, it was through an open tender. My advantage was that I had no freight cost, so I could be 5–10 per cent cheaper than my foreign competitors, which included the Koreans and the Belgians.

Q *Actually this was a very unique set of circumstances and you thrived under this kind of condition when you really bao ka liao?*[13]

A It was based on trust and integrity. Dr Goh trusted me. Now, the roles were totally separated. Mindef did not produce anything. It was left to ST Engineering. As far as I was concerned, these were extra duties for me. I didn't need this damn job. Don't forget, I didn't get a single extra cent. Today, which civil servant does all these things? I would go to CIS in the morning and after I had my lunch at the staff canteen, I would head to Mindef to perform my duties as permanent secretary. And every Saturday, all the general managers (GMs) of these defence companies would line up at my office in Mindef.

They would tell me their problems, which I helped to solve. I didn't run the companies full time. I said, "Okay, see me when you have problems". And I left it to them. I was responsible but I delegated a lot of work to the GMs. I believe in subcontracting jobs. When I got a job from Dr Goh, I looked for someone who could do it and made sure it was taken care of. That was the way I operated. But the difference between us and other countries for defence is that we separated production of weapons from the military. And for convenience, I supervised both.

---

13   *Bao ka liao* is a Hokkien phrase for "taking charge of everything".

Q   *Even though Goh had already left Mindef, he was still actively involved?*

A   He was deputy prime minister and education minister, but he still had oversight of Mindef. One day, he asked me: "So what else do you need?" I told him I have all the anti-aircraft guns and missile defence weapons systems. I needed an early warning system ... the E2C Hawkeye tactical airborne early warning aircraft. He knew what I was talking about. I didn't need to explain. He read all the defence journals. He asked me how many I needed. I said three. He said "two is enough". End of conversation, less than five minutes.

Next day, I *kena*[14] hauled up to Defence Committee of Cabinet (Defco) at the Istana with Prime Minister Lee Kuan Yew, Dr Goh, Defence Minister Goh Chok Tong and Second Minister Yeo Ning Hong. Dr Goh told Mr Lee that I said we needed this E2C early warning radar plane. Mr Lee said yes and asked how many we needed. I said three. Dr Goh said two was enough. I flew to US and bought four. The US aircraft carriers all had four so I believed we needed four. Each aircraft has a six-hour flying limit. And if you buy three and one aircraft goes down for maintenance, you are left with two. So, three can barely cover 18 hours. Israel and Japan were the only other countries with the Hawkeye. Singapore is the only non-alliance country to obtain it. The price was US$601 million. We managed to buy it at US$340 million.

Q   *You were given approval for two but you bought four. Were you reprimanded?*

A   No, nothing. They knew how I was and nobody said anything when I returned with four. Luckily I bought four because one of it crash

---

14   *Kena* is a Malay word which means "to get".

landed when it reached Singapore! I had no personal gain or benefit. What's there to scold?

Q   *Would you say you had a unique relationship with Goh Keng Swee?*

A   He couldn't stand people who were *lor sor*. When I went to see him, I told him what I wanted, he said okay and I *zao*, before he changed his mind. Some people were *lor sor* when they went to see him and he got very fed up. He was most impatient so if you *lor sor* with him, he would get angry, and things would get worse. Some people even tried currying favour with him. Oh, forget it. He had no patience for that. My contact with Dr Goh and Lee Kuan Yew was minimal. I wanted decisions from them, that's all. They knew I would get things done and left it to me. I never sat down and talked long stories with them. I've never been to Dr Goh's house for Chinese New Year or Lee Kuan Yew's house. Never. I only started visiting Dr Goh at his place after his retirement and when he fell ill.

Q   *You had all these successes with weapons. Was there anything you tried making and failed?*

A   Well, Dr Goh was a stingy poke.[15] Once, he asked me: "Why are we supplying the army with vegetables and fruits? Why can't we plant our own pineapples?" So I did. We planted pineapples in Tengah Airbase. But the soil was so lousy that the pineapple was only as big as a hand grenade! We pretty much failed with anything related to agriculture. We tried hydroponics, we failed. Thankfully, we had some success with fruit trees in army camps.

In another instance, he showed me an article in the *Wall Street Journal*, and said: "You see, all these Taiwanese trawlers come to

---

15   "Poke" is a Singaporean slang for "bloke" or "person", often with a negative connotation.

Jurong port at night, bringing in all the fish they catch. There are also blocks of ice with small little *chincalok*, the krill ..." He told me, "Look, all these are free. Why are we buying fish to feed the SAF?" So my staff and I went to Jurong Port after midnight, waiting for the Taiwanese trawlers. Dr Goh was right, there were all those krill and they were being thrown away because it was a waste product. We brought the krill to the SAF Army Catering school and told them to think of recipes using the krill. For one month, the army ate krill, krill egg omelette, until they were so sick of it! We told Dr Goh and he said to stop serving krill. But we had to prove to him that we tried. Dr Goh may seem unreasonable to a lot of people, but he was just very creative and inquisitive. He always wanted to know more and learn more. So the challenge was how you could manage him. If you could convince him with sound reasons and priorities, he would listen.

77

By late 1985, Singapore was deep in the throes of its first post-independence recession, and Yeo had spent some 15 years in defence. Predictably, he was getting restless. Calls were made to him to extend his "extra duty" to the EDB, the outfit which he would become synonymous with for most Singaporeans. Prime Minister Lee Kuan Yew, Trade and Industry Minister Tony Tan and Trade and Industry Minister of State Lee Hsien Loong, who had entered politics a year earlier, all approached him to add EDB to his portfolio. Yeo sought the advice of his mentor Goh, who had just left politics and had become deputy chairman of the Monetary Authority of Singapore. Goh was not in favour of the idea and suggested that Yeo moved to Singapore Airlines (SIA) instead.

Goh saw Lee Kuan Yew and asked for Yeo to be moved to the national carrier. But the premier had other ideas. He called Yeo to the Istana and said: "I know Dr Goh wanted you to go to SIA. We need you in EDB now. You can go to SIA anytime." Yeo's fate was sealed. But he was no longer keen for more part-time work. He asked to be seconded to EDB and in 1986 his tenure with defence came to an end, somewhat. He was asked to continue as head of Sheng-Li, the holding company of the defence firms which would later morph into the ST group. With the EDB job in one hand and ST group in the other, a combination which Yeo referred to as "my two hands", he muscled his way into a new career building the economy, drawing investments and creating jobs.

PART III

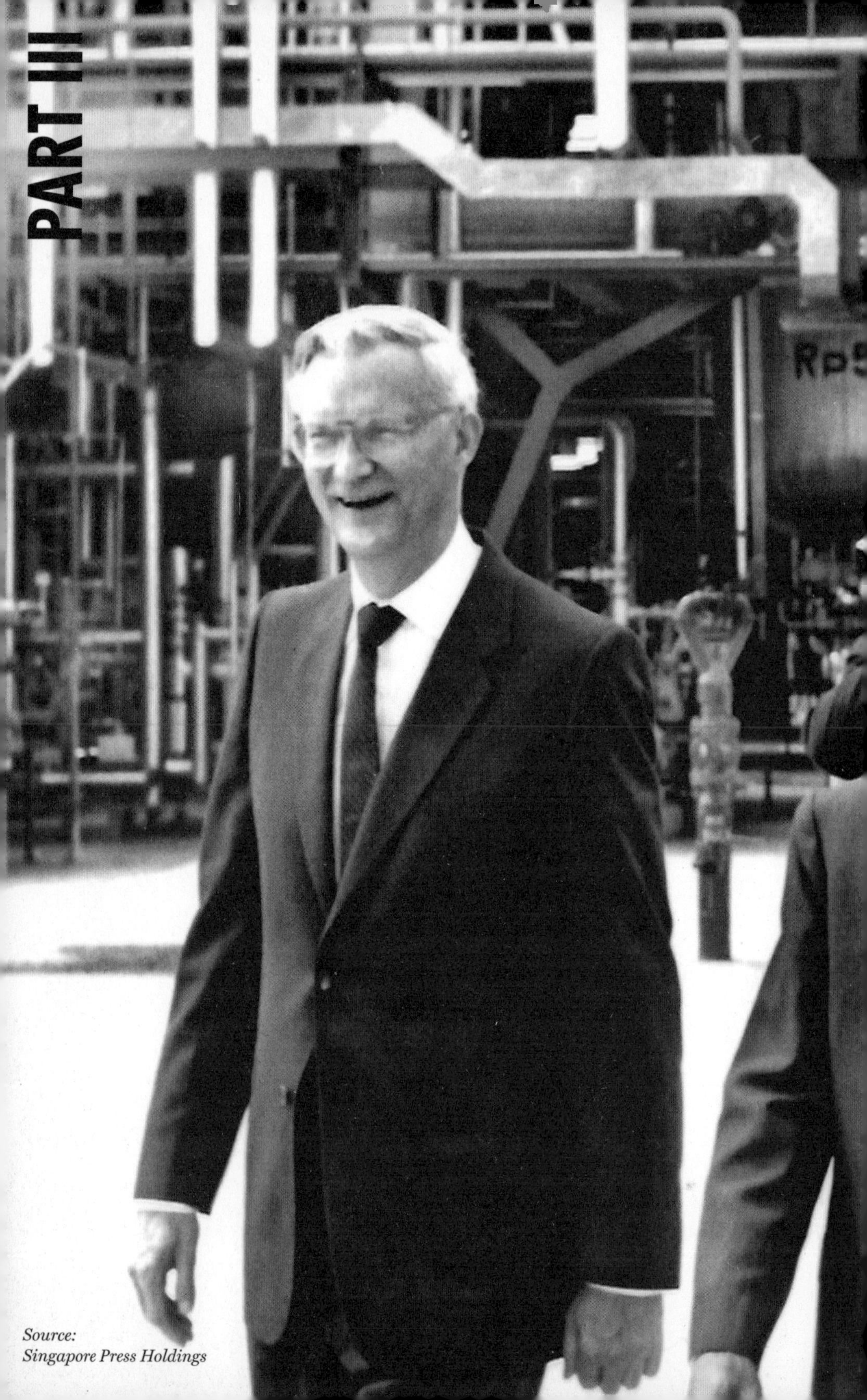

Source:
Singapore Press Holdings

Jobs,
Jobs,
Jobs!

4

Rise of the Economic Czar

"He is truly Mr EDB personified."

S R Nathan on Philip Yeo at the EDB 40th anniversary dinner in 2001

Skies darkened across swathes of central United States. Gale force winds of up to 315 miles per hour left little in its wake. Houses, cars and even people were swept up in one of the worst tornado outbreaks recorded. It was early May in 1999 and 152 twisters were wreaking havoc through much of the country. The ratings for the tornadoes hit the maximum F5. For several EDB officers in the US, their anxiety levels were spiraling out of control too. "The weather was horrendous," remembered Quek Swee Kuan, one of the worried civil servants. "And chairman was stuck in the Midwest." He was referring to Philip Yeo.

Yeo was supposed to be in Boise in northwestern Idaho, headquarters of semiconductor giant Micron. It was a year after the firm had set up its first plant in Singapore and EDB was keen to build on the momentum. But the weather was not cooperating. Thankfully, after a six-hour delay, he managed to catch a flight and landed in Boise at midnight. In a few hours, he had what Quek referred to as a "make or break meeting" with Micron chief Steve Appleton. As Yeo was about to enter the meeting, Quek received the latest information from EDB headquarters in Singapore. It recommended that EDB should take on a higher than usual stake in the proposed new wafer fab facility. Within minutes, Yeo said yes. Appleton agreed too. Eighteen months later, in November 2000, Micron invested S$600 million to build and equip its second Singapore factory in Tampines. It measured 400,000sq ft, or about the size of five football fields. Micron would become the largest employer in the electronics sector in Singapore. "The best salesman was at play," said Quek.

After more than a decade as Singapore's "gunrunner", Yeo went into sales. In January 1986, he was seconded from Mindef to the EDB, starting a new phase in his career that would define not only his life, but also, to a large extent, the shape of Singapore's economy. On paper, the transfer did not seem extraordinary. A ministry's permanent secretary had been moved to head a statutory board. But in reality, the change was drastic. The incongruent civil servant had been released into the jungle of business and entrepreneurship, entering what was likely to be his most natural habitat. He would stay there for 21 years. "People still refer to me as 'that guy from EDB'," he said with his usual broad grin, nearly a decade after leaving the organisation in 2007.

It is not surprising. To many Singaporeans, he became known as "Mr EDB", an economic czar pivoting the country's industries in different directions at various junctures, operating both at home and abroad, moulding the economy to always stay a step, or preferably two, ahead of competition. The length of his tenure is remarkable considering his far from auspicious beginnings in his new job. In 1985, Singapore slipped into recession for the first time since Independence after enjoying two decades of uninterrupted growth, during which per capita income had risen from S$500 in 1965 to more than S$14,000 in 1985. It was a rude shock to Singaporeans. "A bad year meant GDP growth of 5 per cent. A boom year

83

meant 15 per cent growth," said a high-level official committee report formed to relook Singapore's economy. More than 20,000 Singapore workers were retrenched.

Although Goh Keng Swee was not keen for Yeo to move to EDB, it turned out to be an astute decision from Prime Minister Lee Kuan Yew. The board, formed in 1961 to draw investments to Singapore and create jobs, was a lynchpin for the young economy and it needed a fresh impetus to help rescue the economy from the downturn. EDB had been hailed as the "key institution" behind Singapore's economic miracle up till 1985, said Massachusetts Institute of Technology Professor Edgar Schein in his book *Strategic Pragmatism*. But investments in Singapore had stagnated at around S$1.5 billion per year from 1980 to 1985. The EDB, according to Schein, was symptomatic of the Singapore economy's malaise.

By the mid-1980s, EDB had become "complacent and bureaucratic" and had acquired some "dead wood", said Schein. Yeo's entry was meant to shake up the board and, by extension, the economy. He was an unusual choice. The past five EDB chairmen had all spent some of their working career within the EDB. Even though Yeo had been a board member for four years, he had become chairman as an outsider, observed Schein. He added: "The appointment of Philip Yeo as chairman in 1986 was accompanied by a mandate to revitalise the EDB, to reposition its strategy in the new economic context, and to bring back more of the old entrepreneurial spirit."

Yeo, in his inimitable way, was a natural fit. In *Heartwork*, a book on EDB's success, prominent EDB alumnus Ng Pock Too, observed that "whoever leads the EDB must be an entrepreneur, must have a strategic mind, must have guts, must be a strong, tough person and must be a risk taker". Yeo checked all the boxes, said tycoon Kwek Leng Beng. "Philip is an entrepreneur – bold, innovative, challenges convention, highly nimble, disciplined, a risk taker with great tenacity. He has a quantum leap mindset," he said. In one of Yeo's first acts as EDB chairman, he signed off on an advertisement to be placed in the Wall Street Journal. The headline was: "Who would be mad enough to invest in Singapore in a recession?" It carried the signatures of nine global heads of multinational corporations (MNCs), including Apple, Seagate and Motorola, saying "We are", "We are as well", and "So are we". It was his first open embrace of an adjective which he was first labelled with in Mindef, and would be used with increasing frequency by observers in his career. Years later, The Straits Times would introduce his Jurong Island venture with the headline "Mad, Mad, Mad, Mad".

Behind the seeming insanity of the advertisement was a provocative appeal to restore and reinforce investors' confidence in Singapore amid the recession. Manpower Minister Lim Swee Say, an EDB old boy, said Yeo was the perfect man to dig Singapore out of the economic trenches. "The recession was tough, really rough. But you do not fear death when you work with Philip Yeo," he said. "In his lingo, 'we never say die'. No matter how difficult it was, he gave us the confidence that there was always a way out. When there's a big battle to fight, he will be there leading at the front."

It worked. Along with other measures pushed out by the authorities, Singapore rebounded from the recession quicker than expected. By the second quarter of 1986, Singapore's GDP grew by 1.2 per cent and the climb continued to 3.8 per cent in the third quarter. The committee which examined the causes of the downturn, led by then-Minister of State for Trade and Industry Lee Hsien Loong, laid out a plan for the EDB. On top of manufacturing, Singapore would also target services and local enterprises as part of its long-term growth. It also recommended the EDB to move into high value-added industries like chemicals, biotechnology and pharmaceuticals.

Yeo, the new czar of industries, used the blueprint to get to work. It helped that unlike his EDB predecessors, he controlled a vast empire, stretching from the public sector and into the private state-linked companies. He did not function simply as EDB chairman. He moonlighted in other roles too, continuing the "part-time" work habit which he had started since his Mindef days. During most of his EDB tenure, he was concurrently running the Singapore Technologies (ST) group and later on Sembcorp Industries. His experience with ST group, which was diversifying from defence, helped open doors to his new job as the EDB boss. At the same time, his calling card as the Singapore government's representative provided more opportunities for ST group and Sembcorp. The development of Batam is an example (see Chapter 5). "EDB had no resources for a lot of things," he said. "I used all of my Singapore Technologies expense account for my travels and used those trips to take care of EDB's affairs. I was using ST to help EDB. I was a government representative doing business. EDB and ST were my left hand and my right hand." The blurred lines suited the shape shifter perfectly. One could even call it Yeo's modus operandi, similar to that of his defence days, when he was not only the maker, but also the seller and buyer of weapons.

Such ambidexterity helped him achieve his mission: to create jobs. The annual target was 20,000 jobs for Singapore's school leavers. As he said in the EDB 1992–93 annual report: "The charter of the EDB is broad, yet clear – to create good jobs. Economic development means job creation.

Jobs create prosperity and the rest, such as quality of life, will follow. If you have no jobs, there is no quality of life to speak of, no higher standard of living to aspire to." EDB managing director Tan Chin Nam said: "Philip Yeo's mission was very simple – jobs, jobs, jobs." Yeo was relentless in his quest and expected his staff to do the same. He travelled extensively across the world, sold Singapore like "a pimp" (in his own words) to multinational corporations and worked tirelessly to find jobs for Singaporeans. "He was probably the best travelled chairman EDB ever had. He never stopped," said David Lim, another well-known EDB old boy, before repeating to emphasise his point. "He never stopped." Yeo said he was hardly in Singapore. "I didn't spend much time in the office. I was on the road most of the time," he said.

He expected the same of his staff. Lim Swee Say recalled a conversation Yeo had with a young staffer in the US: "He asked the young man 'Do you know why we have to walk so much on the road? When you're tired, when investors scold you and when you feel discouraged, always remember why you are doing this. It is to create good jobs for Singaporeans.' For other leaders, the focus may be on drawing more investment dollars. Not Philip Yeo. For him, the reason for our work was always about creating good-paying jobs for Singaporeans." Years later in 2007, when Yeo became the chairman of SPRING Singapore, an agency to help small and medium enterprises (SMEs), his mantra on jobs remained unchanged. "When Philip Yeo talks about helping SMEs, he says we're not doing it to make the *towkay*[16] richer so that the *towkay* can buy another house or another car. It's because SMEs employ many Singaporeans," said JTC Corporation's CEO Png Cheong Boon, former CEO of SPRING. Yeo's job-creation efforts were

87

---

16   *Towkay* is a Hokken word for "boss".

recognised by Singapore's labour movement in 2008, when he was awarded its Distinguished Star Award.

EDB officer Quek, who is now the CEO of Sentosa Development Corporation, recalled another anecdote of Yeo's uncanny salesmanship on the road. In July 1998, Stephen Luczo was made CEO of data storage firm Seagate, a company which had significant investments in Singapore. He was not familiar with Singapore and EDB, and Yeo had never met him before when a meeting was scheduled in December 1998. "We went into the meeting cold," said Quek. But as Yeo strode into his office in Cupertino, California, he noticed a row of familiar monster action figures. "Pokemon," Yeo thought to himself, recognising right away the icebreaker he needed with this new boss of the Fortune 500 company.

"What is this? You're playing Pokemon?" asked Yeo.

"It's my nephew. I've got to play with him and I keep losing," said Luczo.

"My daughter plays Pokemon," said Yeo, who shared the battle tactics of the Japanese game and urged Luczo to read Pokemon's strategy guide book.

They spent almost the entire meeting discussing Pokemon, exchanging tips and trading tactics, to the amusement of the watching EDB officers. Said Quek: "How Chairman knew about the Pokemon strategy guide, I don't know! After the meeting, on Chairman's advice, we went to pick up the Pokemon guide and delivered it to Steve's office shortly after the meeting. The relationship with Steve was strengthened from then on."

The years in EDB earned the famously amphibian Yeo a surprisingly sticky title – Chairman. His subordinates called him that, and many of the EDB alumni, or "EDB mafia" according to former chairman Chan Chin Bock, continue to address him by that honorific. Yeo, in typical self-deprecating humour, preferred to call himself a "hustler", a "pimp" or even a "concierge". He explained he would do anything to service a client, hence the label of a concierge.

In 1995, for instance, clothing firm Levi Strauss sent an American to head its new Singapore office. But the transfer hit an unexpected bump. The incoming CEO's children were upset when their pet dog was impounded and quarantined by the Singapore authorities for months. The kids were crying. Levi Strauss' headquarters called Yeo to complain. Yeo called Primary Production Department (PPD), present day Agri-Food and Veterinary Authority (AVA), and made a "polite urgent request" to the department director. "Release the bloody dog!" he urged. PPD refused, but allowed the children to see the dog and cut short its quarantine. "This is customer service, total service, concierge service," said Yeo. "Even a dog became my problem. But we needed the investment, so it's okay. I would do anything to get the deal over the line."

Beyond the personal touch – he knew most of the CEOs personally – his larger strategy was to group EDB into four main clusters of industries – electronics, precision engineering, chemical and biomedical sciences. Previously, the board ran operations from project to project, with little connectivity in between. Yeo wanted his officers in each group to not only build up expertise in each industry, but also generate a family of businesses related to each other, or what he called "Christmas trees". In short, create a cluster.

For example, instead of just promoting computer disk drives, the cluster would also look to bring in companies producing the mechanical parts that go into the disk drives. In this way, the disk drive firms would find

89

component parts in Singapore, accentuating the allure of the country as an investment destination. The idea came from Yeo's military days. "In defence, every industry has a group. When you make guns, it is mechanical forging, so that includes coins like what we did for Chartered Industries of Singapore," he said. "When I made a rifle, I would need spare part components. So I needed a supporting industry."

A key upside to having these clusters is a back-up whenever an industry slides. Instead of betting big on just one sector, the strategy spreads out the chips on multiple smaller punts. Yeo is a strong believer in the perpetual motion of industries. "No industry lasts forever," he said. He has a 5-5-5 rule. Every industry struggles through its first five years, grows and stabilises in the next five and then matures in the last five. By the second fifth year cycle, it is time to rejuvenate or move on. "You must bring in new clusters every five to 10 years, otherwise it's not sustainable," he said. Kodak, for instance, has gone from a genericised brand to bankruptcy because of its failure to adapt to the digital revolution.

The cluster idea was behind one of Yeo's most risky ventures – Chartered Semiconductor Manufacturing. As he was bringing in American semiconductor firms to Singapore using his EDB arm in the mid-1980s, he recognised an opportunity for his ST group arm. He started Chartered Semiconductor to produce wafers, the highest productivity end of the industry. In good times, the value-added per worker could hit as much as half a million US dollars per worker a year compared to less than US$100,000 a year for semiconductor assembly and testing. But it was a high investment and high risk business. That didn't deter Yeo. Chartered Semiconductor's first wafer fabrication plant was set up in 1988 at a cost of more than S$300 million. But by 1991, the global semiconductor industry had hit a massive recession, and the company's losses racked up to more than S$100 million. ST group's top decision-makers were divided on whether to keep faith with the new venture or cut its losses.

Yeo, as ST group executive committee chairman, and a team of fellow believers including Singapore Technologies Ventures (STV) executive president Ho Ching, asked for a S$70 million capital injection to expand capacity. They believed the problems were cyclical and short term. By growing its output in this downturn, it would help the company be commercially viable, he argued, driving down unit costs to a more competitive level. But the call was akin to "waving a red flag before a bull", said *Towards Tomorrow*, a book on ST group. The ST group board was divided on whether to support further investments. Yeo staked his future and reputation on it. "I asked the ST group board: 'What do you want to do with this company? If you don't want it, sell it to me. I will take 60 per cent and you can take 40 per cent," he recalled in Towards Tomorrow. "I will resign from government service tomorrow morning and I will run it." The board blinked first in the brinksmanship and gave its approval. Yeo and Ho and the believers were proven right. By end 1992, Chartered Semiconductor started to break even and it was listed in 1999 with Temasek, Singapore's state investment firm, remaining as its largest shareholder. By the time Chartered Semiconductor was sold to Abu Dhabi in 2009, it had risen to become the world's third largest chip maker.

To drive his "two hands", he relied heavily on getting good men and women. Former army chief and JTC Corporation CEO Lim Neo Chian, who has worked with Yeo since his Mindef days, said "people development" is probably Yeo's most enduring legacy. And it was at EDB that his life-long interest in building talent took on a clearer shape and character. It was also at EDB that he developed scholarships in a big way, solidifying a love affair with the financial aid award which would subsequently make him a household name in Singapore. Some 15 years after he first pooled together the systems engineers in Mindef, he would gather a fresh gang in the EDB. "I don't believe in charters, hierarchies, or layers of seniority. I believe the best and brightest can do the job. So my fundamental concern is how to create enough young talent, and I spend most of my time looking for good people," he said in the book *Strategic Pragmatism*.

Once he took over as EDB chairman, he quickly added 38 senior investment promotion officers and doubled the offices overseas from 18 to 37. He also managed to get the Public Service Commission to "donate" a few of their newly-returned scholars to the board. For good measure, he brought over three officers whom he was familiar with: Tan Chin Nam; David Lim, who joined politics later as a Cabinet Minister; and Thong Pao-Yi, who rose to the rank of Executive Director of Communications of EDB. All three were from the National Computer Board where Yeo was chairman from 1981 to 1987. "He gave me a file to read, asked me to see him at EDB and when I turned up, he told me that's my room," said Lim, laughing. "And just like that, I was in EDB. He never discussed it with me. I was conned."

Yeo made it clear he wanted the best people. As he explained in *Heartwork*: "You meet the CEO of a top-10 company in an industry, and you tell him it's a good idea to stake his credibility and sink in millions of dollars of investment on a piece of rock nearly 10,000 miles away. The only proof of claim we offer is that we will treasure the investment and hopefully become so profitable, it could become the best investment they ever made. Therein lies the challenge of every EDB officer: how to convincingly "hustle", sell and bring investments into Singapore."

The criteria was simple yet difficult to fulfil. They must be passionate, courageous and able to take hard knocks. "We needed officers with the canine tenacity of a bulldog, the sweet eloquence of the nightingale, and the stamina of a stubborn buffalo to keep knocking on doors, never say die, always confidently persuading, negotiating and convincing the investors to invest in faraway Singapore," he added. "We needed officers with a passion to succeed for Singapore. It was true then and it will always have to be for the EDB to succeed, and for Singapore to succeed."

It is perhaps not a coincidence, given his military years, that the phrases used by his EDB folk are borrowed from the same lexicon. Those who actively market Singapore are called "road warriors", the ones based overseas are "field officers" and the anecdotes they share are "war stories". They had to be fast, adaptable and strong. "Many young officers half his age could not catch up with him, both physically and mentally," said former EDB managing director Ko Kheng Hwa. Former Cabinet Minister George Yeo described Philip Yeo as a "blob of mercury" when he was on the road. "Now here, now there," he said, having travelled with him extensively during their Mindef years. "You don't get to do sightseeing. So when you travel with him, it's all work. You see hotel room, you see meeting rooms, then you're on the way to the airport, to the hotel, and to the airport again. But it was interesting."

Failure to keep up with Philip Yeo's punishing pace could be perilous. "I tell you, it was so exhausting. He walked so fast, you know?" shared EDB alumnus Khoo Seok Lin. Once, for instance, Yeo and Lim Swee Say were queueing up for their boarding passes at an airport in Chicago. He asked a young officer accompanying them to get three hot dogs from the nearest food stand. "Swee Say and I got our boarding passes in less than 15 minutes, then we went looking for our missing officer," said Yeo at a dinner in 2013. "We found him at the hot dog stand – patiently putting ketchup, onions, condiments, et cetera, et cetera onto the three hot dogs! I expected him to bring the three hot dogs 'naked' to us. The officer failed the hot dog test. No more future trips with us." It was also important for an EDB officer to know where to find good Asian food around the world. "One of the core competencies of an EDB officer in the field is to know where to find the best Teochew *mee pok*[17] in Paris," said Ko with a straight face. "Or dim sum, or wanton noodles. After a business dinner meeting eating the Western stuff, Philip must have his noodles." Even in Sweden, said Khoo. "He hates Western food."

Officers, whom Yeo usually referred to jokingly as his "slaves", were expected to be ready for curve balls thrown their way too. A favourite "war story" of the EDB mafia came from current EDB managing director Yeoh Keat Chuan. In 1996, he was in Taiwan with Yeo to meet the boss of chemicals firm Chi Mei. During the meeting, Yeo suddenly told the Taiwanese boss, who could only understand Mandarin and Hokkien, a southern Chinese dialect, that the young Singaporean would give a presentation in the dialect. Yeoh, who is of the Hokkien dialect group, was stunned. But he gamely soldiered on. "I remember describing EDB's industry cluster development strategy, but since I didn't know the Hokkien word for cluster, I used "bunches"

---

17   *Mee pok* is a type of flat yellow noodle of Teochew origin. It is a staple in Singapore's hawker centres.

instead!" he said. "Chairman also engaged the Taiwanese boss in Teochew which is similar to the Taiwanese Hokkien. I thought he appreciated it and we built up a good rapport." The story became "part of the aura" around Yeo, said Khoo, enhancing his reputation not only as a leader but also a salesman. In 1996, the Asia Times called him "Singapore's ace salesman" in a profile, and Fortune magazine said he "probably knows more CEOs of major corporations than anyone else in Southeast Asia". Those who are close to him are in no doubt of the strength of Yeo's reach. "The power of his network is amazing," said National Gallery Singapore's CEO Chong Siak Ching. "I believe that no person on earth cannot be reached by Philip or through any one of his contacts."

The Philip Yeo brand of insanity drew as many critics as adherents. Current EDB chairman Beh Swan Gin said that there are many from the EDB alumni who regard themselves as "Philip Yeo loyalists". "We did our best to support him in whatever it was that he put his mind to," he said. "It wasn't just about obligation because we benefited from him ... it's (about) the leadership values that we learnt from him, because he was one boss who backed you, who gave you autonomy. He'd been right many, many more times than he had been wrong and his intentions had always been for the good of Singapore, for advancing Singapore's cause. So it's very easy to be a Philip Yeo loyalist."

In 2010, in a replica of the famous Wall Street Journal advertisement, his officers past and present put together a mock advertisement with the headline "Who would be mad enough to work for Philip Yeo?" There were 13 signatories, including then-labour chief Lim Swee Say, David Lim, Tan Chin Nam, politicians Josephine Teo and Lee Yi Shyan and JTC chairman Manohar Khiatani among others. They were all part of Yeo's EDB mafia.

95

Q *You were a very active chairman. Did you change the role of the EDB chairman?*

A Yes, it's my character. I can't sit in the office. When I was in Mindef, you hardly saw me there. Most of the time I was out. I was running defence companies in the morning, out in the factories and also overseas procuring weapons. So Howe Yoon Chong liked to make fun of me by asking, "Are you coming or going?" In Edgar Schein's book on EDB, he said that it is a very strange organisation, where the chairman is practical and the CEO is strategic. Chin Nam likes management theories.

Q *So you reversed the roles of a chairman and a CEO?*

A Yes, you could say that. I became the hands on guy, always flying, always on the move and always meeting clients. Chin Nam ran the operations at home in the headquarters.

Q *How did EDB adjust to your new style?*

A They had to follow. Everywhere I travelled, I brought one young officer and the officer would stay with me for one whole week. If we were heading to Japan, we would leave on Sunday night, take the "red-eye" flight and reach Tokyo on Monday morning. I would head to the toilet at the airport, change my clothes, grab breakfast on the go and make my way to the city for meetings.

Q *You didn't check in your baggage?*

A   No, we just *tarik*.[18] It's a waste of my time waiting for checked-in luggage. I just squeezed all my clothes in.

Q   *For an entire week? Do you wash your underwear in the hotels?*

A   No need. One week is five working days, so I needed five shirts, five pants, five pairs of underwear. That's all. In those days, airport security was relaxed so when you have no checked-in luggage, you can get out of the airport very quickly. When I first got to EDB, the officers all brought big bags on our trips. But the moment we landed, I would walk out of the airport while the silly ones were still waiting for their luggage. I would say, "Goodbye to you". On the next trip, no one would check in any luggage. They all followed me.

Q   *How hectic was your one week overseas?*

A   The day I touched down, I would start my first meeting at about 8am. I would have had five to six hours of sleep on the plane, so what's there to complain? I wanted to make sure that my one week on the road was most effective. I would work from Monday to Friday, morning till night. Every day, there would be a briefing over breakfast, followed by two meetings with companies before lunch. After lunch, there would usually be another meeting with a client. If there was no business dinner, we would take a little break. At 10pm, there would be a debrief of the day in my room. There were usually five to six meetings a day. On Friday night, I would fly home to spend the weekend with my family.

Q   *What about in the US?*

Q
&
A

97

---

18   *Tarik* is a Malay word which means "pull". In this instance, he was referring to cabin-size luggage.

A   I usually chose to land in the east and moved west. I would arrive on Sunday and start working on Monday. A typical day trip would be New York, Delaware, Chicago and then Los Angeles. I would have 27 hours flying from east coast to west coast because the west is three hours behind the east. We ate at airports, usually hotdogs and salad. Once, we packed it so tight that even then-Deputy Prime Minister Lee Hsien Loong had to run in the terminal to catch the flight. To be fair, he never complained. He knew how we worked. Four cities, east to west, one day, it's not so difficult.

Q   *How is that possible? No flight delays?*

A   In those days, before September 11, it was easy. We had no baggage to check in, so we just walked right up to the gate. There were no security checks like what we see today. Osama bin Laden created TSA (Transport Security Administration).

I remember once, I was in Boston or New York and I received a distress call from Chuck Haggerty, chairman of Western Digital, the big computer data storage company. Haggerty said he was sending a guy to run the operations in Singapore but he didn't want to go because his kid couldn't get a place in the American School in Singapore. I told him to wait for me. I flew to Irvine, California, and called the principal of the Singapore American School and put him on speaker in front of Haggerty.

"This is Philip Yeo here, I am with the chairman and CEO of Western Digital," I said. "His officer is being posted to be CEO of their operations in Singapore and he is not going because his kid cannot get a place in your school."

"Ya, but, Mr Yeo, we've got a long queue," said the principal.

"I don't give a damn. Jump the queue."

"Okay, Mr Yeo. We will do it."

Q   *You knew the principal?*

A   He knew me. I didn't know him. Chuck Haggerty was there and that was how he respected me.

Q   *What kind of argument was that? You just said 'I don't give a damn'?*

A   I was a bully. I bullied him. I needed the investments. Singapore needed the investments. I needed the Western Digital guy to be here in Singapore.

Q   *What if the principal had said no to you?*

A   They all knew my reputation. They knew my holy anger.

Q   *Everyone associates you with EDB. But are you the sort of guy who is interested in economics?*

A   Well, I don't see it as economics. I look at it as job creation. I'm not your theoretical kind of guy. I don't really care about the structure of the Singapore economy, because to me, the structure is provided by the companies. What we provided were land, educated people, utilities, water. It was up to the companies to decide what industry, what business and what they wanted to do. I don't see Singapore as a normal national economy. We're a city state. So we really have no domestic market to encourage them to come here. Not like China or India. So really, we are dependent on the global market. A big company, a multinational, will look at the market and decide on its business and products. What I wanted was to provide a home for them, a place for them to operate.

Q *But in deciding which company to attract to Singapore, in a way, you are determining the structure of the economy?*

A In a way, yes. For example, in 1986, we decided to go for all the disk drive companies. The good thing about disk drives is that they need a lot of mechanical components. Many of the manufacturers of these components were local companies. In less than two years, we created 40,000 jobs. Then I realised that, look, besides making the mechanical parts, the key part of the disk drive is also the component and the memory chips. So I promoted semiconductor. In a sense, semiconductor complemented disk drive.

For the companies, they required components. Whenever a cluster was created, they came. They knew they could easily get key component supplies in Singapore. Even when they are competitors, they would come here because they all want the same components. It's a bit like, when you think of electronics, Sim Lim Square comes to mind immediately. The key was that when I was building any industry, I tried to build it as a group rather than just individual companies. This was how we built the economy. We have no oil, we have no land, we have no customers. But each company has its own global customers and after producing here, the companies ship their products to the rest of the world.

Q *What were some of your selling points when you met these MNCs?*

A We gave them tax holidays, we gave them full and complete support and we found them workers. We helped them with workers' training. We subsidised the training. We were almost in hospitality mode. EDB functioned like a hotel, offering Singapore-style hospitality. Look, we have no great natural wonders. We have nothing. We are a base for them to produce and ship their goods everywhere. We're the gateway, we're the bus stop, we're the bus terminal. That should be the way, right?

Q *What happens when the tax holidays end?*

A We came up with the idea for tax holidays tied to products. So as long as you bring in new products to Singapore, you get a new tax holiday. We moved the tax incentives from company specific to product specific. The MNCs were all very happy. This also meant they had incentives to bring in new products to our country. So firms like Hewlett Packard, even though it has been in Singapore for many years, has never paid a lot of tax. Same for Glaxo.[19] Every new drug they brought in, they got a new tax break.

My thinking is that with every new product, you deserve a new tax break because you are creating jobs. And there is also indirect income for the government through other taxes, property and employment. So the government has nothing to lose. And don't forget, when the companies come here, they put the cash here, so Singapore also benefited as a financial centre.

Q *Mention Philip Yeo and EDB and chances are, Singaporeans would think of "scholarship". Can you share how you got started on scholarships in EDB?*

A The best way to develop people is to take them young. Under EDB, the moment you had a scholarship, you were required to come back to work at EDB every school holiday. By the third and fourth year of university, the person would be well exposed to what kind of work EDB did. My idea was that I should give out enough scholarships

---

19 Glaxo is a global pharmaceutical company. It is now known as GlaxoSmithKline.

to replace the existing EDB officers in 10 years. But the government refused to give me money for scholarships. So I went around begging. So Japan's ISK, a chemical firm, gave me one scholarship. Every Japanese company gave me one or two scholarships.

But the big one came in 1989. I was having dinner with Sir Paul Girolami, Chairman of Glaxo, which invested in Singapore in 1982. He spent the evening telling me how happy Glaxo was with the Singapore operations.

"Philip, what can I do to thank the Singapore government?" he asked.

"Sir Paul, why don't you create a Glaxo scholarship?" I suggested. "We give 30 of Singapore's brightest young students each year a chance to study engineering at the best universities in the UK and the USA. And they will carry the Glaxo name."

"How much do you want?"

I took a pen and did a quick calculation on a dinner paper napkin. "Well, 30 students a year multiplied by 10 years is 300." So I calculated and said about S$50 million. He was amused, said okay immediately and set up a $50 million trust fund. He didn't ask any questions. He went back and sent me two cheques, S$25million each. We didn't exchange any memos. That was how it all started. The first batch of EDB-Glaxo scholars left for their studies in 1990. Later, other investors also sponsored scholarship programmes, including Mobil, Seiko-Epson, Takashimaya and some Singapore companies too.

After I got more and more scholarships, the PSC asked me if I could stop because my scholarships bypassed them. I gave scholarships under my own terms, with six-year bonds unlike theirs which were eight years. I said my guys had to finish National Service so six years was enough. So eventually PSC followed me.

By 1988, Singapore's Fixed Asset Investments (FAI) in manufacturing's new projects crossed the S$2 billion mark for the first time. In 1994, FAI crossed S$5 billion. In February 2001, Yeo left EDB for the National Science and Technology Board, the present day Agency for Science, Technology and Research (A*STAR), retaining only supervision of EDB's biomedical sciences cluster as co-chairman of the board. The FAI then was S$9.2 billion, just shy of the S$10 billion target he had set for himself.

The foreign investments brought in by EDB contributed to a robust Singapore economy through the 1990s. But it was not without problems. Soon after the country rebounded from the 1985 recession, it became obvious that wages were rising without sufficient improvements in productivity. The economy's competitiveness was again under threat and Yeo heard the top guns of MNCs complaining openly about labour shortage. If they were unable to expand, they would move out of Singapore. Yeo was flummoxed. It never occurred to him that the solution would be an island that is a 30-minute boat ride away.

103

5

Wind Beneath the Second Wing

"If we don't go regional and sprout the second wing, our destiny will pass us by."

Lee Kuan Yew in a parliamentary speech, 1994

When an Indonesian ambassador to Singapore asked Philip Yeo to build an industrial town on a Riau island near Singapore, the civil servant replied: "What is Batam?" Despite just a 30-minute speedboat ride away, most Singaporeans, like Yeo, had never heard of the island. But Yeo's curiosity was piqued by that conversation in March 1989. He quickly made a visit, as always, and realised his year-long search was finally over. He had finally found the place that can help Singapore sprout its "second wing".

The rebound from the 1985 recession was so swift that it took the Singapore government by as much of a surprise as the downturn. By 1988, job losses had been replaced by labour shortage and foreign workers, primarily from Malaysia, had to be brought in. When foreign labour curbs were subsequently introduced, MNCs and local enterprises were desperate for an outlet to expand. One could say it was a happy problem, preferable to retrenchments. But it required a solution nonetheless. Yeo, as EDB chairman, sought the advice of his mentor Goh Keng Swee.

While Goh had retired from politics in 1984, he had taken up the role of deputy chairman of the Monetary Authority of Singapore (MAS) and was still eager to help his protégé. "We sat in his office at MAS discussing Singapore's economic predicament for well over an hour. Dr Goh was one of those rare people who knew how to hold my attention on a single topic for so long," Yeo recounted in *Heartwork*, a book on EDB's successes. Goh's suggestion to solve the labour crunch was to look overseas. Find a location that would allow MNCs in Singapore to split up their operations. The labour-intensive work would be taken abroad, while their high-value work could remain in Singapore.

Yeo started scouting but was increasingly frustrated. He explored the possibility of Malaysia, looked into Thailand and even considered China. But they were all unsuitable. Johor at the southern tip of peninsula Malaysia was the most obvious choice. It is connected to Singapore by a bridge and ticked all the right boxes in Yeo's checklist. "My rule of thumb was: if I wanted to assemble something, I wanted it to be nearby," he said. "I could assemble, I could bring back, then ship it out using Singapore as my hub. The most logical choice was Johor." But the high toll fees between the two countries and the frequent congestion dampened his enthusiasm. "It's such a hassle to go to Johor," he said. Add to that the awkward politics between Singapore and Malaysia, two nations which were once in a short-lived merger, and he gave up on his first option.

An earlier experiment in Ayudhya, Thailand, petered out after differences with the locals, so Goh urged him to look farther north. Goh was appointed economic adviser to China's State Council, or its Cabinet, for its Special Economic Zones in 1985 and he urged Yeo to check out the southern Pearl River Delta. Cheap labour was in abundance but Yeo was not keen. China was too far from Singapore for companies based in the city-state to split their operations without significantly increasing costs. When the bloody Tiananmen incident happened in June 1989, with student and other civilian protesters gunned down, Yeo was quietly relieved he did not, for perhaps the first time in his career, follow Goh's advice.

Batam? Yeo might not have heard about it but was soon attracted. "Small jetty, lots of virgin jungle, not much by way of industry except for McDermott in the oil and gas supply business. The island was well connected by good roads, newly built. There was one freshly-painted traffic light and one petrol station for the whole island," wrote Yeo in *Heartwork*. "The location was almost perfect. This was an untouched island, only half an hour away by fast ferry. It was better and much nearer than the other sites we had seen. On a clear day, I could actually see it from my 25th floor office in Raffles City Tower." He loved it. But there was a problem. He was the only one who did. Goh rubbished the idea and said: "You are crazy. They have been trying to do this in Batam for many years." Apparently, industrialising Batam had been part of the Indonesian government's plans since 1975. But very little headway was made. The late Wong Kok Siew, who was Yeo's classmate from St Joseph's Institution and his right-hand man in Singapore Technologies (ST) group, complained loudly to his colleagues: "He's crazy. This is Philip Yeo with another crazy idea!"

But the madness, which was fast becoming the buzzword of Yeo's career, turned out to be quite a sound idea. The Batam experiment was a defensive move despite its seeming offensive appearance. Yeo needed to find affordable labour for the investors in Singapore so as to prevent them from uprooting their operations altogether. "Otherwise, sooner or later they would move because they couldn't get labour," he said, and Singaporeans' jobs would be lost. This strategy dovetailed neatly with the government's plans to venture aggressively overseas.

In 1990, during a trip led by Deputy Prime Minister Lee Hsien Loong, the Singapore delegation was introduced to the "*shakkei*" concept in Kyoto. It meant "a beautiful garden is made more beautiful by integrating distant scenery into the garden landscape", wrote Chan Chin Bock in *Heartwork*. He added: "This concept provided the inspiration for a small country like Singapore to leverage on the resources and attractiveness of its partners to achieve collective competitiveness. A limited Singapore can therefore become 'Singapore Unlimited' and this is the basis for globalisation and regionalisation for Singapore."

The new administration under Prime Minister Goh Chok Tong was determined to take Singapore's economy outward, calling it the country's "second wing". The first was the domestic economy. Fortune magazine summed up the expansion in 1996: "By cloning itself overseas, Singapore intends to forestall any large-scale exodus among those 3,000 multinationals now there. Its hope: As their overall Asian business grows, foreign corporations will maintain and perhaps expand their regional headquarters in Singapore – and even keep open existing factories, if only to train managers and workers bound for the new plants abroad." As Prime Minister Goh, who succeeded Lee Kuan Yew in 1990, said in a parliamentary speech in 1994: "Singapore is right in the midst of this booming region. Go out and seek your fortunes."

Yeo would become a key driver, or a strong gust of wind, beneath this "second wing" through the 1990s. While he had been familiar with foreign markets when drawing investments to Singapore and procuring weapons

107

for the military, that work largely revolved around imports, whether in foreign direct investments (FDIs) or arms. But this new phase would see him exporting the Singapore model, sinking roots abroad in a manner which he, or Singapore for that matter, had never done before. He was blessed to again have his "two hands" for this new adventure. He drove the strategic thinking behind the industrial parks in his role as EDB chairman, but executed its construction and its management through the ST group vehicle which he headed. He would go as far as to say that without the dual roles, he could never have succeeded overseas. He could never have helped transform hitherto little-known foreign towns into household names in Singapore: Batam, Bintan, Wuxi, Suzhou, Bangalore and Binh Duong. But the first, and still closest to his heart, remains Batam.

The project bore all the hallmarks of a Philip Yeo special. It slashed through bureaucratic red tape, circumvented proper channels and was built with frightening speed – even by efficient Singapore's standards. Five months after Yeo first visited the island, then-Prime Minister Lee Kuan Yew formally proposed the idea to his Indonesian counterpart President Suharto. In 10 months, the deal was inked. In 16 months, Lee and Suharto officiated at the topping-up ceremony of the industrial park's first factory block. By the 22nd month, in January 1991, consumer electronics giant Thomson started operations, producing TV remote controls. The time it took from conception to operation was less than two years. "His speed was both to chase the opportunity and also an awareness that speed allowed him to overcome some of the problems that he would face inadvertently," said EDB alumnus David Lim. "He likes to say it's easier to get forgiveness than to get permission." Yeo admitted as much. "My philosophy is that if I do things fast, very few people would dare to oppose me. They can't catch up," he said.

He gave Goh Keng Swee a lot of credit for Batam's success. Despite the retired politician's initial misgivings, he gave his support quickly and visited Batam two months after Yeo first broached the topic. Yeo showed him the location, a jungle in the middle of Batam, near two large bodies of water. It was called Duriankang by the locals because of the durian trees in the area. It was the perfect site for Yeo, a durian lover. He recalled his conversation with Goh in Batam.

"Good idea. What are you going to do?" asked Goh.

"I want to start work now," Yeo replied.

"How can you start work now? You need to have a proper G to G (government to government) agreement."

109

"What is G to G? I have never dealt with Indonesia. What do I have to do to get G to G?"

"You have to write an aide memoire for PM Lee to take up with President Suharto."

"What's an aide memoire?[20] What do I write?"

"I will write it for you."

Goh wrote the aide memoire, asked Yeo to check the facts and personally brought the note to Lee, who broached it with Suharto in August 1989 and the Indonesian leader gave his approval. This despite Yeo's two demands – tax holidays and 100 per cent ownership by MNCs of their investments – being largely alien to Indonesia then. When Yeo had to visit Jakarta to pitch the idea to Indonesian ministers, he cajoled Goh to join

---

20 "Aide memoire" is a diplomatic term for a proposed agreement.

him. "He looked at me and said 'okay, but you pay.' He's a stingy poke," said Yeo with loud laughter, clearly enjoying the recollection despite telling this anecdote countless times. Goh's words to the Indonesian leaders helped Yeo move Batam quickly. "He told them, 'Philip Yeo wants everything done in two years. He is not a patient guy,'" said Yeo.

The warning was served. Yeo started work in February 1990 with no land title, no permits and little funding. Indonesia's Research and Technology Minister B J Habibie, who also oversaw Riau and later became president of Indonesia, asked him: "Pak Philip, you've got no land title, no permit." Yeo replied: "You are my land title." Given the bureaucracy and corruption in the country, the Singaporean knew that slowing down could derail the project. "I knew that waiting for the land titles would mean months of inaction. I moved so fast the Indonesians could not cope. They didn't know what to do," he said. He didn't even have sufficient money when the groundbreaking ceremony took place. "I needed to borrow money and Indonesia's interest rate was 20 per cent!" he said. He asked Goh for help again and the mentor issued a letter as deputy chairman of MAS, authorising him to borrow $500 million from Singapore banks.

The banks, with the exception of the now defunct Overseas Union Bank, were not supportive. Singapore government had neither the experience nor the knowhow to pull off an industrial park overseas. Yeo admitted that if a feasibility study had been carried out, the project would have been deemed non-feasible. Singapore Technologies Industrial Corporation (STIC) president Wong Kok Siew, who had initially thought the Batam idea was mad, said people told them: "You guys went in because it's national service." But "that was a lot of bull", he told *The Business Times* in 1993. "We went in because we saw an opportunity." Yeo stressed that the Singapore government did not put in a single cent for the Batam project.

A joint venture company was set up, with Indonesia's Salim Group holding a 60 per cent stake and STIC 40 per cent. To draw investors, Yeo relied heavily on his EDB contacts. In February 1990, he escorted Sumitomo Electric Industries chairman Tetsuro Kawakami around the barren site. "I will build you a factory in this jungle, and I will have it ready within one year," he pledged. The Japanese took him at his word and he delivered. In February 1991, Sumitomo moved into its new Batam factory. Said EDB officer Khoo Seok Lin who worked on the project: "The ordinary person sees it and thinks nothing. Philip Yeo sees an empty land and dreams big things!" More tenants arrived, including a stellar blue-chip cast of companies such as Philips, AT&T, Seagate and Sanyo. The division of labour between Singapore and Batam also took off. Thomson, for instance, moved its labour-intensive assembly work to Batam but left its high-value work, such as the production of its TV tuner, in Singapore. The goods made in Batam were also shipped out of Singapore, bolstering the city's port.

The project, which is known as Batamindo Industrial Park, was a runaway success. Within three years, it was returning profits. The projection was five to seven years. Even Yeo was surprised. By 1996, five years after the park started operations, there were 84 international companies in it. It generated US$950 million worth of exports that year. In 2014, it was US$2.75 billion. Along the way, it swept Singaporeans into a brief but memorable Batam craze in the 1990s. Weekend trips to the island were frequent, with golf, shopping and seafood dining the most popular activities. Singaporeans even tuned into two popular Batam English language radio

111

stations – Zoo 101.6 and Coast 100 – and pushed out Singapore stations. For a people more accustomed to looking north for business, industry and leisure, it was a dramatic shift southwards. More critically, the park gave Singapore a breathtaking opening chapter in its pursuit of success stories in regionalisation. "The development has helped Singapore as a whole, to open up a second wing in its economic development phase at that time," said Goh Song How, former managing director of the park. "This pioneer experience allowed many others to start their integrated industrial township development in the subsequent years."

Yeo would take the same model and adapt it with varying success in Bintan in Indonesia, Bangalore in India and Binh Duong in Vietnam. In India, for instance, the authorities had wanted an industrial park in Bangalore, modelled after Batam. But after surveying the landlocked city, Yeo realised it would be logistically challenging to have a similar export-oriented production-based industrial park. Instead, he suggested building the country's first information technology (IT) park. Indian conglomerate Tata Group, which would partner a Singapore consortium in the project, was sold on the idea. "Philip's plans always seemed to make good business sense," said Ratan Tata, who was chairman of the Tata Group. "Most of the senior civil servants in Singapore are very professional and very efficient. Yet, Philip differentiated himself as being a person in a great hurry to get things done, a friendly yet demanding executor, a person with tremendous vision. Everything he has done in Singapore and every task he has been given has been executed with amazing clarity and great vision." Three years after inking the deal, Siemens Semiconductor became International Technology Park Bangalore's first tenant in 1997. In 2005, Tata and the Singapore investors profitably exited the project and transferred their stakes to JTC's subsidiary Ascendas.

But Singapore's second wing, at least on those flights piloted by Yeo, would experience significant headwinds in China. It started well enough with Wuxi, a town in Jiangsu province by the lower reaches of the Yangtze Delta. Goh Keng Swee had urged Yeo to replicate Batam in Wuxi and, after the Indonesian park was operational, Yeo obliged in 1993. The vision was similar – a self-contained industrial park with foreign investments creating jobs for the locals. But unlike Batam, the Wuxi project was not an official government-to-government collaboration. Yeo used his STIC vehicle to build the Wuxi-Singapore Industrial Park on a purely commercial footing. "I never asked the government for help. I was perfectly happy working on Wuxi," he said. He managed to start construction of the Wuxi project six months after negotiations first started.

Storms blew in from a neighbouring Chinese city. Running parallel to the Wuxi project was a bigger and more famous tie-up between Singapore and China. In 1994, under the supervision of then Senior Minister Lee Kuan Yew, the two governments committed to build an industrial township in Suzhou, another Jiangsu city and just an hour's drive from Wuxi. The project was not commercial. From its inception, it took on a clear political agenda. Lee wrote of his proposal in his memoirs *From Third World to First*: "A government-to-government technical assistance agreement to transfer our knowledge and experience (what we called "software") in attracting investments and building industrial estates, complete with housing and commercial centres, to an unbuilt site of about 100 square kilometres." In short, said Lee, the idea was to create a "miniature Singapore" in Suzhou.

113

Yeo was not initially involved in the Suzhou Industrial Park, or SIP. But when the first masterplan for the park was ready in 1994, Lee summoned him to the Istana, where Lee's office was located. Yeo recalled the meeting:

"So what do you think?" asked Lee.

"Very few brown spots," replied Yeo.

"What do you mean 'brown spots'?"

"Industries. Brown for industry. There's less than 15 per cent, maybe 10 per cent. Where are the jobs?"

Lee, according to Yeo, was surprised. The plan was to locate 600,000 people in the town and yet there were not enough jobs to sustain this population. The elder statesman was livid, called for a meeting the next day with the officials involved and gave them a shellacking. "Philip Yeo says this is wrong," said Lee.

"All of them got a real scolding. He used my name, sabo me," said Yeo, using a colloqial contraction for "sabotage". "Lee Kuan Yew was really angry. The meeting was over in a few minutes and nobody dared to answer him. He walked to his office, huffing and puffing." Yeo left the meeting relieved. "Oh, I was very happy," he said. "The project had nothing to do with me. I walked out a free man." It was premature elation.

A year later, in late 1995, reports from Suzhou spelt trouble. The project was not moving and the Chinese were unhappy. EDB managing director Lim Swee Say, who was sent by Lee to survey the project, reported back that it needed help. "One day Mr Lee Kuan Yew asked me, 'so what is the so-called bottleneck in Suzhou now?'," recalled Lim. "I said 'We need help. We need to bring industry players into Suzhou. And the best person who can make it happen is Philip Yeo.'" Lee did not waste any time. He called Yeo at 10pm and wanted to see him the next day. Yeo was given the mandate to take over as chairman of the joint steering committee and overhaul the team.

Yeo handpicked EDB old boy David Lim to go to Suzhou as CEO of the SIP, followed by a group of officers from the EDB mafia. One of them, Josephine Teo, who is now a Senior Minister of State in the Cabinet, said Yeo spared no effort to make the project a success. "He brought the full force of the EDB to bear and during that period of time, so many EDB centre directors visited Suzhou so that they knew their investment product as hustlers," she said. "Our officers were out there trying to promote Suzhou, trying to tell people how this industrial park was different from anything else."

Yeo focused on only 1,000 hectares of the land – or 10 per cent of the total project – and aggressively lured MNCs to Suzhou. "I was looking at industries, at jobs. The others like housing can come later. The key was jobs. It's always about jobs. Batam, Bintan, Wuxi, it's all about jobs." It worked. The likes of Hitachi, Siemens, AMD, Eli Lilly, Nabisco and Samsung moved into the SIP. Said Lim Swee Say: "Philip Yeo may be unhappy, but once he gives a commitment to a project, he makes it happen. That's what I respect about him."

The problems with the local Chinese officials did not abate. Lee wrote about the difficulties in his autobiography: "Instead of giving SIP their full attention and cooperation as was promised, they used their association with Singapore to promote their own industrial estate, Suzhou New District (SND), undercutting SIP in land and infrastructure costs, which they controlled. This made SIP less attactive than SND."

Yeo was outraged with the local officials' diversionary tactic. "I was

115

very pissed off. So one day I told them I was very angry with them because of all the problems. I said, 'I bring you investments, I bring in know-how, I bring you jobs, I bring you exports, and here you are screwing me?'," he said, raising his voice as he bounced momentarily off his seat with fury at his own recollection. The anger, delivered in English to the Chinese officials, was translated by his special assistant Seah Kia Ger from EDB. "Kia Ger translated in a very nice way. I knew it because I was looking at their faces and they were still smiling. When I scold someone, his face usually turns pink." Seah, a Nanyang University graduate, laughed when recalling those meetings. "Philip would hustle me to scold them harder. But it was enough. The Chinese got the message," he said.

The Suzhou project started the wrong way, said Yeo. It made two critical mistakes. First, instead of setting up shop in the Suzhou New District as the local officials had recommended, Singapore selected another place to build its miniature Singapore. "Big mistake. I told Lee Kuan Yew that we should never have taken that place," said Yeo. In Wuxi, he built the industrial park in the zone chosen by the Chinese cadres. Second, Singapore took a majority stake of 65 per cent in SIP, with the Chinese having 35 per cent. "We got 65, they got 35, why should they cooperate with us? My rule is always the other way round, unless that guy has no money in the first place," he said. "At SIP, they get 35 cents for every $1. At SND, they get the whole dollar."

By 1999, despite Lee's raising the problem with Chinese President Jiang Zemin two years earlier, the problem in Suzhou was not resolved. Yeo had had enough. After a meeting with Lee, where Yeo said there was nothing more he could do, Singapore and China agreed to swap their shareholdings. Lee called it "a chastening experience" in his autobiography. Yeo just wanted to forget about his nightmare years overseeing the SIP. His antipathy showed in his writings and interviews. He almost never ever mentioned Suzhou. In his farewell speech from A*STAR in 2007, Suzhou had a blink-and-you-miss-it mention when he looked back at his career. "It was intentional. I didn't want to get involved. I never asked for this project and never wanted it. I did it for Lee Kuan Yew's sake. I'm not proud of this project," he said.

Q *What would have happened to Singapore if it didn't help develop Batam?*

A Sooner or later, many of the MNCs would have left. They would have to. They could not have developed their entire value chain in Singapore because we would not have enough labour for them. Eventually, many did leave. But having Batam helped buy us time. It allowed the companies to move their labour intensive operations, especially the assembly work, to Batam while the rest remained in Singapore. Batam gave us more time as we changed our economy.

Q *Why was it important to buy time?*

A No industry lasts forever. Remember my 5-5-5 rule? Every five years, you have to start planning for a new industry. For me, it was important to buy time during the transition of industries because I had to think of the workers. For a worker who is 50 years old, if I can help buy 10 more years in his industry, it would mean him keeping his job until he is 60. He won't face retrenchment in his 50s and struggle to make a living after that. Every industry shift affects many people. The job of an economic planner must be to think of such consequences. How will our decisions affect the lives of the people?

Unfortunately, Admin Officers (AO) today don't understand that. Such thinking is alien to them because they will be in a job for three years, transferred to another post and then they *zao*, all gone. They are moved before the shit hardens. It's a very big serious issue. When I was chairman of EDB for 20 years, it was my job to worry about industries and jobs for the next five, 10 and 15 years. If I were an AO today, staying in a position for three years and then moving on, do you think I give a hoot? I made this comment when speaking to AOs at the Civil Service College and they all looked at me funny. I said you guys never sit there long enough. You don't have to worry about the hot seat. Maybe that's why they never invited me back again.

Even ministers move, move, move. So now the backside moves and the head moves too. Where you sit affects how you think, right? Once you're given the job, if you don't sit there long enough, why should you care? It's not that you don't want to care. But it's just not your worry. It's the next guy's problem. It's the same for the People's Action Party (PAP). The PAP has been around for 50 years, so they worry about the next five, 10, 15 years. If there is a new government every five years, then *bo chap*, because the leaders may not be around anymore. That's called democracy.

If a government doesn't have long-term tenure, it will not take a long-term view of things. I spent 15 years in Mindef. I worked on weapons way before anybody else because I have to think of many next years. But if I'm in Mindef for only two or three years, you think I give a damn? The next posting, I'm gone.

Q   *Some critics have argued that Batam could not sustain its success and started to go downhill after 2000. What is your response?*

A   The Asian financial crisis in 1997 and the fall of Suharto in 1998 changed things in Indonesia, including Batam. From 2000 onwards, Indonesia became out of control in terms of labour action. In 1990, when we started the project, there was only one national union in Indonesia, similar to Singapore. After 2000, every 50 workers could form a union. Strikes became more common. Batam gave Singapore 10 good years from 1990 to 2000. I'm very happy and satisfied. Beyond that, what can I do?

A few years ago, the Indonesian government invited me to give a presentation to its ministers. My first powerpoint slide was a big crocodile. The next slide was a little crocodile. What's the point of the crocodiles? In the old days when there was one big crocodile, he bit you but still delivered. Things got done. The country is a democracy now, with a lot of players, a lot of small crocodiles. Every little crocodile bites you, takes your money but never delivers. Nothing gets done. The Indonesian officials laughed. They had a sense of humour. They said: "Pak Philip, you're very frank." And that's the problem with Indonesia today – too much democracy.

Q *Do you feel upset that for a lot of Singaporeans today, Batam is often associated with a sex visit?*

A What to do? It's not my fault. I've done my share. I created jobs, that's it. I moved on. Once, I was on my way to Batam on the ferry with two of my lady staff. The ferry was full of Singapore taxi drivers going there for the weekend and they were looking at my two girls. So I told them: "They think you are new shipment!" I used to visit Batam almost every month. I would meet the workers there and talk to them. I told you about the condom story, right?

Q *Condom? No, you didn't.*

A You don't know the story?

Q *No.*

A When I first built the industrial park, I looked all over Indonesia for young people aged 18 to 24 who finished high school with 12 years of education, and could understand English. We built dormitories for them inside the park. It was mostly assembly work and we employed largely women. The ratio in the park was four girls to one boy. An Indonesian minister told me jokingly that this was heaven! We separated the girls from the boys in the dormitories. All fenced up. The rule in the park was that they have to stay single during their three-year contract because we had no housing for married couples. So if the girls got pregnant, they had to leave and be sent home. But they were young women and there were young men, so what do you think was going to happen?

One day, this girl got pregnant. She hid in the toilet, used a cloth to tie around her stomach to abort the baby. The baby died. She nearly died too. I rushed over to Batam, called the workers and scolded the managers. How did this happen? What's the solution? I told them to put condoms in the medical centre and make it available. The Indonesians looked at me, stunned. A foreigner was telling them to put condoms in a Muslim country. "You want to be responsible for another death?" I asked them. So they listened to me and it was done. No more deaths.

Q *Doesn't that suggest the initial rules were overly stringent to begin with?*

A I didn't come up with the rules. Look, to me, they were 18 to 24, what do you expect them to do? If they couldn't do it in the dormitory, they could go to the park, to the town, anywhere. There's no way to stop it. It's against human nature. I was worried about the girl's welfare. She could have died. I told the Indonesian minister very clearly: "I don't want another death." But the Indonesians were very practical and they accepted it. At most they said Pak Philip was a crazy guy. But they knew I was concerned about them and they listened.

Q   *How did you get them to listen to you?*

A   I spent a lot of time on the ground with them. I visited them, made sure the dormitories were good, and made sure food was good. When the first bunch of workers started working, they got their monthly salary in cash and put it under their pillows. The money was stolen. So I quickly got three banks to open branches in Batam, and all the companies were told to pay the workers through the banks. All the workers had bank accounts. They had never had a bank account in their lives. So every month on salary day, the workers would queue up at the banks to check their statements. They were *kiasu*.[21] They wanted to make sure the money was in their accounts. It was interesting. We built a clean, organised and safe industrial park. It was almost like an army camp. I guess it must be my Mindef influence?

Q   *How did the Batam project lead you to Bintan too?*

A   The Indonesians were very pleased with Batam and so they invited us to develop Bintan too. Bintan has a long shoreline with beautiful long beaches. The Indonesian navy used to practise amphibious landing there, making Singapore navy very worried. The development in Bintan was largely in tourism, just a little bit of industries. We built resorts and golf courses. I wanted it to be a resort for visitors to Singapore. Most of the time, when foreigners came to Singapore, there was nothing to do but work. There was no place to relax. I thought Bintan could be that relaxing place for foreigners to take a break from the fast pace of Singapore.

Part of the agreement on Bintan was also to negotiate water supply from Riau for Singapore. There is a mountain in South

---

21   *Kiasu* is a Singlish term that means "afraid to lose out".

Sumatra, with 4,000 million gallons of water every day. Most of it flowed right into the sea. Wasted. Our government wanted to take the opportunity to buy water from the Indonesians and my idea was to build a dam, create a reservoir and transport the water to Singapore. In 1991, we signed the agreement to pump 1,000 million gallons of water to Singapore every day, for 100 years.

Q   *But this agreement was never implemented?*

A   It moved very slowly and died after the financial crisis and due to Indonesia's political uncertainties. Also, there were concerns that building a pipeline from Bintan to Singapore would be very costly. Singapore also managed to move into Newater and desalination, so there was less urgency to buy water from other countries.

Q   *Let's talk about a project which you are less enamoured of: the Suzhou Industrial Park.*

A   When I took over in 1996, I was up there in Suzhou every two, three months. I was on the road to bring in investments, to build the factories. I never had dinner with the Chinese. I never *yam seng*[22] with them. Anyway, I can't drink. Alcohol sends me under the table. Every time I was there, it was for business. And I made sure that once I finished my meetings, I would fly home. I was not known for hospitality. I didn't believe in all this *wayang*.[23]

Q   *I thought you said you were a concierge of Singapore?*

A   Only if I wanted something out of them. Haha. Kidding. But I was really pissed off with the Chinese. I was very unhappy. They were

---

22   *Yam Seng is a* Cantonese toast. Yeo was referring to having drinks with the officials.
23   *Wayang is* Malay for "theatre performance". It is used colloquially to mean "play acting" or "an act of pretense".

screwing us, dragging their feet over everything, like land transfer. And they would steal from me. I brought Motorola in, and they stole Motorola from me. I told people that my first project was in Wuxi and it's my first wife. I was very happy and contented with my first wife. Then I had to abandon her to take care of this stupid woman called Suzhou. Usually the concubine is better than the first wife, right? But not in this case. I disliked the concubine. The Wuxi people, my first wife, were very sad when I told them I had to go to Suzhou.

Q   *What did Lee Kuan Yew have to say about your unhappiness?*

A   He knew, he knew. I told him the Chinese were stealing my underwear.

Q   *I'm sorry?*

A   Yes, I told him that the Chinese were stealing my underwear all the time. You steal my shirt, that's okay, I've still got pants. You steal my pants, that's okay, I've still got underwear. If you steal my underwear, I will have nothing left. I have no dignity. You don't give me any face. He understood. He didn't get angry with me. He didn't say I was rude. He knew I was mad. Then he said: "So what should we do?" I said to withdraw. Give them the majority. His words were: "So when will you do it?" I said: "Now."

In 2002, the Chinese ran a full-page advertisement on Suzhou Industrial Park in the *Financial Times*. Absolutely no mention of Singapore. The complete name of the project is "China-Singapore Suzhou Industrial Park". But they dropped "China-Singapore". The ad listed all these companies, most of which were brought over by Singapore. But where's the credit? No other country has done this to me. I bought two copies of the *Financial Times* and sent one to Mr Lee. I told him I didn't want to have anything to do with the project anymore. After that advertisement, I wanted nothing to do with them.

Q *But your problem was with Suzhou and not with the Chinese. You had a good experience in Wuxi, didn't you?*

A In the Suzhou case, we started on the wrong footing and with the wrong concept. It was all wrong. My job was to repair. But it was too much for me. When Lee Kuan Yew announced they were going to Suzhou, Dr Goh (Keng Swee) called me up. He said: "This project will fail and they will call for you." He was against the concept from the beginning. When we went to Wuxi, for instance, it was purely commercial.

But yes, I actually enjoyed working with the Chinese before the Suzhou project. When Zhu Rongji[24] was mayor of Shanghai in the late 1980s, he came to see me in Singapore and wanted me to brief him on EDB and our economy. When one of his senior guys asked the same question he had raised earlier, he turned to him and scolded: "You are not listening!"

Q *He's a bit like China's Goh Keng Swee.*

A Yes, he is. He just *bo chap*. So after I briefed him, I hosted him to dinner. After dinner, I asked him if he wanted to look around Singapore since it was his first visit. So we took them to Newton Circus[25] and I still remember we bought him durians and coconuts. He asked me to look at Pudong[26] in Shanghai. He wanted to sell

---

24 Zhu Rongji would rise to become Premier of China, serving from 1998 to 2003.
25 Newton Circus is a popular food centre in Singapore near its main Orchard Road shopping belt.
26 Pudong refers to a district in Shanghai, east of the Huangpu River. It was largely made up of farmland until rapid development in the 1990s transformed the area into Shanghai's industrial, technological and tourism hub which hosted the World Expo in 2010.

me land in the high-tech industrial zone. But it was very expensive and we couldn't afford it. I still remember Lee Kuan Yew scolding me years after that. We made a mistake by not taking up the offer. Anyway, I took care of Zhu when he was a mayor.

Q *You don't speak Mandarin. How did you converse with Zhu?*

A We spoke in English! His English was quite good. His wife spoke to me in English too. All discussions were in English. Years later, when Lee Kuan Yew found out I knew Zhu Rongji, he asked me how we communicated. He was very surprised when I told him we spoke in English. Mr Lee knew I refused to learn Mandarin. When we had problems in Suzhou, Mr Lee asked me: "Can you go and talk to your friend?" He was referring to Zhu. He's a friend, you see.

126

Q *How big a role did personal relationships with foreign leaders play in your ventures overseas?*

A Ultimately, it's all about people, it's about relationships. The Indonesian officials are my friends. When Habibie made a movie, he sent it to me on a DVD. He sent me his book too. When his mother was very sick, I arranged for her to seek treatment at Mount Elizabeth hospital in Singapore. Every night after work, I would go with him and his wife to the hospital, have dinner and discuss his mother's illness.

When the Indonesians visited Singapore on private trips, they gave me a call and I would meet them. If they asked to see a doctor in Singapore, I would arrange for them, for their wives, for their mothers. It was usually medical related. I was their concierge. To the Indonesians, I'm their friend, so it's normal for me to help them. Now, which EDB chairman would do that? Which permanent secretary would do that? Which Singapore minister would do that? None.

When their children got married, they would invite me and I would attend the weddings. I attended Habibie's son's wedding, Tunky's son's wedding, Radius' daughter's wedding.[27] No Singapore leader attended. After I left EDB, no one from EDB attended such weddings anymore. When I go to Jakarta, I have no problems seeing them. I had no problems getting things done for Singapore.

Q   *Are the relationships still active today?*

A   Well, I was in Jakarta to see Luhut and he wanted me to help with the Riau project.[28] He's trying to see if we can get it going again. He's not familiar with anybody in Singapore so he asked to see me. As far as Luhut is concerned, he trusts me. Indonesians are like that, you know. They trust you, they like you, they work with you. It's not about the rank.

Q   *So if you were tasked to tackle the haze problem today, what would you do?*

A   I would go to Jakarta now and speak to Luhut first. "Hey, you want me in Riau, Batam, Bintan? You better do something about the haze." He would listen to me. Personal relationships are important, but they take time to cultivate. Singapore officials no longer take time to develop deep personal ties with officials in other countries.

---

27 Tunky Ariwibowo, Minister of Industry for Indonesia under Suharto, was a key official in the Batam project. Radius Prawiro was the Coordinating Minister of the Economics, Finance and Industry and Development Supervisory Board in Indonesia. Both officials have passed away.

28 Luhut Pandjaitan is Indonesia's Coordinating Minister for Political, Legal and Security Affairs. He is the most senior Indonesian official in charge of tackling the haze crisis. He was a former Indonesian ambassador to Singapore from 1999 to 2000 when he worked with Philip Yeo.

Singapore's "second wing" ambitions continued to grow despite setbacks like the SIP. For example, in 2008, the country started a second "government to government" project with China at the northern port city Tianjin. The new project is an eco-city, taking the industrial development of the SIP a few steps forward by emphasising sustainable growth. In 2015, it was announced that a third Singapore-Sino project will be launched in Chongqing, western China. For Singapore government-linked companies such as CapitaLand and Ascendas-Singbridge, the overseas market has become de rigueur. Aided by the growth of the Internet and budget carriers, the external scene has meshed so naturally with Singapore firms today that it is no longer seen as an unknown frontier. Perhaps it is the best compliment to the phrase "second wing" that it has long slipped from not only official speak, but also laymen talk.

128   For Yeo, the overseas ventures are a key part of his legacy. "Regionalisation was really pushing this idea that we cannot just think within our borders," said current EDB chairman Beh Swan Gin. "If we want to grow the economy, we have to think about how we are able to leverage on the resources of other countries and establish win-win partnerships to do that. So Philip Yeo was always ahead of his time. And that's why he's so impressive as a leader. Today, I'm trying to resuscitate, not even start, Batam, and it's hard work ... and he did not only one, but multiple at one go."

Yeo never stopped his push overseas. In 2013, he set up his own company, the Economic Development Innovations Singapore (EDIS), exporting Singapore's successful economic model. Projects include places as diverse as Colombia, Brazil and Kazakhstan. But more on EDIS later. Amid his "second wing" adventures abroad, Yeo never forgot home. In the early 1990s, he came up with the most ambitious, and yes, craziest, idea of his life.

Left: Gene and Elaine, 1990.
Source: Philip Yeo

Above: Eugene Yeo Wei-Ming, 23, has been
chosen to receive the Lee Kuan Yew Scholarship
on 5 June 2000.
Source: Singapore Press Holdings

Right: Elaine with MAD ads.
Source: Philip Yeo

Family portrait, 2000. *Source: Philip Yeo*

PETER TAN

dancer with the Singapore Dance Theatre, 27. Single

A powerful dancer with grand leaps and immense energy. Even when he's not dancing, he's moving all the time. A compact bundle of hard muscle from years of lifting female partners. Small-framed — he's 1.71 m — but has a washboard-hard tummy. And a smile as sunny as an afternoon in Sentosa. He definitely puts a spring in your step.

BERVYN LEE

teacher, 27. Single

A rare man who knows his Shakespeare. One of a new younger breed in his profession, he proves that teachers aren't all stuffed shirts — nor are male teachers all wimps. Earlier this year, he was one of a team of teachers who made their rounds of schools encouraging students to take up teaching as a career. Has a sense of fun but at Anglo-Chinese Junior College, he's a no-nonsense discipline teacher.

KOH BOON PIN

speech trainer, 28. Single

A little-boy-lost in person, a gripping actor on stage. He relishes taking diverse roles. From a tormented man who turns into a cockroach to a coolie Chinese coolie fresh off the boat arriving in America. He has a wonderful voice with perfect diction and crisp, clear tones — if you're fussy about phonetics, he'll never let you down.

PHILIP YEO

dynamic Economic Development Board chairman, 45. Married (Right)

He's Supermind. 1990's Business and Industry Personality of the Year is a living example that you don't have to score an A in looks to be sexy. Said Patricia Scherschel, former editor of Singapore Business magazine: "He's got a mind that races ahead at 80 km per hour. A man who seems able to think on two tracks at one time. He's bursting with ideas."

KELLY CHAN

Singapore's top board-sailor, 34. Married (Far right)

Craggy good looks and terrific tanned torso from all those hours at sea. Sweet-natured, he's been married for 14 years.

Facing page: Philip Yeo was voted as one of Singapore's sexiest men by Her World in 1991.
Source: Her World © 1991 SPH Magazines Pte Ltd. Reproduced with permission
Top: Philip Yeo with his son, Gene, and daughter, Elaine. *Source: Philip Yeo*
Bottom: Elaine's MA Psychology Boston College graduation. *Source: Philip Yeo*

Family portrait, 2016
Source: Economic Development Innovations
Singapore (EDIS). Photographer: Kua Chee Siong

Highest honour for outstanding efforts: Philip Yeo (right) being conferred Indonesia's Bintang Jasa Utama on 19 July 1994. *Source: Singapore Press Holdings*

Left: Philip Yeo (Chairman, EDB) receives the prestigious National Order of Merit from the French Ambassador Francois Barry De Longchamps on 3 October 1996. *Source: Singapore Press Holdings*
Right: Philip Yeo and Lim Siong Guan receives the Order of Nila Utama (First Class) from President S R Nathan at the Suntec City Ballroom. They were among 350 recipients of National Day awards honoured in 2006. *Source: Singapore Press Holdings*

(Left to right) Japan ambassador to Singapore Makoto Yamanaka, Philip Yeo (Chairman, SPRING Singapore) and Shu Tamaura (Second Secretary, Japan embassy) at a ceremony where Philip Yeo was conferred the Order of the Rising Sun, Gold and Silver Star in recognition for his contributions to bilateral relations and cooperation between Japan and Singapore on 19 December 2007.
Source: Singapore Press Holdings

Top May Day Award winner 2008, Phillip Yeo, 61, receives the highest honour for a non-unionist, the Distinguished Service (Star) award. He was one of two who were given top honours in the National Trades Union Congress (NTUC) May Day Awards which are bestowed on persons and companies that have made significant contributions to the Labour Movement.
Source: Singapore Press Holdings

Philip Yeo being conferred the Honorary Doctorate of Engineering by the University of Toronto in 1997. *Source: Philip Yeo*

Philip Yeo being conferred the Honorary Doctorate of Science by the Imperial College London, United Kingdom in 2007 for being one of "Singapore's true pioneers of economic development in harnessing Singapore's skills in industries such as semiconductors, aerospace, specialty chemicals and biomedical sciences". *Source: Philip Yeo*

Philip Yeo being conferred the Honorary Doctorate of Law by Monash University of Australia in 2011. *Source: Philip Yeo*

Philip Yeo being conferred the Honorary Doctorate of Letters by the National University of Singapore in 2011. *Source: Philip Yeo*

Philip Yeo with Lee Kuan Yew at Asian Aerospace in 1988. *Source: Economic Development Board*

Philip Yeo (third from right) with Mr and Mrs Lee Kuan Yew on a visit to Jurong Island on 13 January 2001. With them are (left to right) Chong Lit Cheong (CEO, JTC); Lim Neo Chian (Chairman, JTC); Teo Ming Kian (Co-chairman, EDB) and Ko Kheng Hwa (Managing Director, EDB). *Source: Lee Kuan Yew, Senior Minister's Office.*

Philip Yeo and Jane Yeo with Lee Kuan Yew at The Order of Nila Utama (First Class), National Day Award ceremony in 2006. *Source: Philip Yeo*

(Left to right) Lua Cheng Eng (CEO, NOL Group) and Philip Yeo (Chairman, Sembawang Corporation) with Lee Kuan Yew (Senior Minister, Singapore), who launches the commemorative story of Sembawang Shipyard, *Of Hearts and Minds*, by pushing a piloting device lever in 1998. *Source: Singapore Press Holdings*

Wee Cho Yaw (Chairman, United Overseas Bank) (right) shaking hands with Anthony Salim (Salim Group) at a signing ceremony yesterday for the massive industrial park in Fuqing city in China. Also at the ceremony were (from left) Philip Yeo of the Singapore Technologies group, former Deputy Prime Minister Goh Keng Swee and Chinese ambassador Zhang Qing.
Source: Singapore Press Holdings

Arriving in Indonesia, (left to right) Barry Desker (Ambassador to Indonesia, Singapore), Philip Yeo (Chairman, EDB) and Goh Keng Swee (Deputy Chairman, Monetary Authority of Singapore) at the topping up ceremony of Batam Industrial Park, Indonesia in August 1990.
Source: Singapore Press Holdings

(Left to right) Howe Yoon Chong (Minister for Defence, Singapore), Goh Keng Swee (Deputy Prime Minister, Singapore), Lai Chun Loong (General Manager, CIS) and Philip Yeo (Second Permanent Secretary, Mindef.), circa 1981 at an annual Chartered Industries of Singapore (CIS) showcase of new development products. *Source: Lai Chun Loong*

Goh Keng Swee at the launch of the EDB book *Challenge and Response: Thirty Years of Economic Development*. Goh supervised the book which was written by a group of NUS lecturers and economists. *Source: Philip Yeo*

Visit by Philip Yeo, Second Permanent Secretary to the Ministry of Defence to 3 SADA at Seletar Camp MHB R182(27A). *Source: Ministry of Defence*

Government officials and representatives from the private sector at the press conference to explain the implications of the report of the Committee on National Computerisation in 1981. They are (from left facing camera): Tan Chin Nam (Director, Systems and Computer Organisation, Mindef), Lim Choon (Deputy Director, Manpower Planning and Education, Ministry of Trade and Industry), Foo Meng Tong (Administrator, Skills Development Fund), Ong Wee Hock (Deputy Director, EDB), Robert Iau (President, Singapore Computer Society), Philip Yeo (Second Permanent Secretary, Mindef), Lau Ping Sum (MP, Yio Chu Kang and president, Data Processing Managers Association), Hsu Loke Soo (Head, computer science department, NUS), and Wang Mong Lin (Director, CDIS, Ministry of Education). *Source: Singapore Press Holdings*

FRONT ROW SEATED (LEFT TO RIGHT): Lta. Tan Yew Thiang (INSTR), Lta. ...
Lta. Sim Wah Kwong (INSTR), Lta. Chua Jang Sioe (INSTR), 2Lt. Seah Beng L...
OFFR), Mr. Wong Kok Siew (HD. ORG & CONTROL), Mr. Philip Yeo (DR. FINAN...
(INSTR), Lta. Pang Kim Foung (INSTR), 2Lt. Koh Cher Wah (COURSE LEA...
Yong (INSTR),

BACK ROW (LEFT TO RIGHT): 2Lt. Lee Sin Chong, 2Lt. Beetama GJ. Louis, 2...
Chan Chin Yong, 2Lt. Gwee Teck Gee, 2Lt. Oh Teng Leong, 2Lt. Chew Cheng ...
2Lt. Andrew Chia (COURSE STUDENT REP.), 2Lt. Ng Weng Kit, 2Lt. Leong Ka...
Eng Leong, 2Lt. Henry Koh, 2Lt. Lim Hong Leng, 2Lt. Lim Choon Lock, 2Lt...
2Lt. Ong Joon Juan, 2Lt. Yeo Eng Liang, 2Lt. Leo Teng Hui, 2Lt. Lim Hong Li...
Absent: 2Lt. Denis Choo.

FICERS COURSE (3.1 C)

OCT. 73.

ui Leng (INSTR), Lta. Richard Tan Keng Hee (INSTR),
T. PERS. OFFR), Cpt. Goh Kim Chwee (CHIEF LOG TRG
DMIN), Mr. Low Ah Tee (DY. DR. SOLA), Cpt. J. Isaac
Lta. Lim Kian Hoe, Lta. Ee Cher Neo, Wo1. Kang Ai

Ing Yew, 2Lt. Ng Ngee Ley, 2Lt. Lee Ser Chye, 2Lt.
t. Tan Eng Lai, 2Lt. Au Tai Tuen, 2Lt. Jee Loy Thong,
2Lt. Ong Lian Kee, 2Lt. Daniel B. Stanley, 2Lt. Lian
ong Sin, 2Lt. Tan Seng Hui, 2Lt. Goh Peng Whatt,

PHOTOGRAPHER
Bobby Yip
TEL: 54494

Source: Philip Yeo

P. D FIN — seen 3/6.

MINDEF PS 0024/70 Vol II

31 May 76

MINDEF Directors of Divisions

The following changes in appointments will take effect from Monday, 14th June, 1976:-

(a) Mr Lim Siong Guan, Director Logistics, to be Director Finance

(b) Mr Philip Yeo, who has just returned from his MBA Course in Harvard, will take over as Director of Logistics

(c) Mr Goh Kim Leong has been awarded a PSC scholarship to do a MSc Programme in Business Administration in September 1976. Pending his departure, he will be available to assist both Director of Finance and Director of Logistics.

(Pang Tee Pow)
Permanent Secretary
(Defence)

Distribution:

List A

List B

List C

List D

List E   Dist J
          D/F
List F   H.Adm
          H.IA
          H.A
          H.B
          H.CPB
          H.VSB
          SAF Pmr
          C.FC(L)
          C.FC(A)
          C.FC(S)

Mindef Directors of Divisions,
31 May 1976.
Source: Ministry of Defence

Address: "SINGDEF, SINGAPORE"   MINISTRY OF DEFENCE
Ref: Tanglin
Ref: REPUBLIC OF SINGAPORE   Singapore 10

14th January, 1976

Mr Philip Yeo Liat Kok
3 Peabody Terrace
Apt 22
Cambridge, Mass. 02138
USA

Dear Philip

    I returned to Singapore on Christmas eve after spending three days in San Francisco visiting our pilots in Lemoore. The Navy liaison man came promptly at 10.30 am to Baker Hall to fetch me to the airport. I was not able to contact Koh as our telephone lines were promptly cut off on the 19th December. Koh himself did not contact me. I hope you had a pleasant holiday in New York.

2   Could you let me know the postage charges for the parcel which you sent for me? So far, I have not received the second parcel which was sent in November from Boston. Hope to get it any time now as it is about 2 months since it was posted.

3   Minister has asked when you will be finishing your course and I told him that you will be coming back some time in June. He has directed that you should come back immediately after the course as your services are urgently required in MINDEF. Please let me know when you are expecting to complete your examinations and the likely date that you will be back here.

4   Please convey my regards to your wife.

Yours sincerely

(Pang Tee Pow)

Letter from the Permanent Secretary of Defence on 14 January 1976 to
Philip Yeo conveying Goh Keng Swee's directive to return to Singapore
immediately on completion of his Harvard programme. *Source: Philip Yeo*

The industrial engineering way to the top

Industrial engineering is a good bet for anyone aspiring to do well either in the public or private sector, contends Colombo Plan Scholar Philip Noel Yeo Liat Kok.

His performance in the civil service bears ample testimony. He began his career in the service with a Bachelor of Applied Science (Hons) in Industrial Engineering from the University of Toronto, Canada, in June 1970. Today, he is one of the high flyers in the service. At 32, he is the Second Permanent Secretary in the Ministry of Defence and is chairman of three government-owned companies and executive director of another.

He said: "In industrial engineering, we do have a good dose of basic engineering studies, like thermodynamics and fluid dynamics. However, the speciality of this course is the emphasis on management studies, computer science, and operations research. This is obviously the ideal course to pursue in view of the current trend of drafting engineers to perform administrative jobs."

Indeed, a 1977 national survey of engineering manpower showed that 54% of local engineers were performing managerial functions. The University of Singapore's Engineering Faculty is now revising its curriculum to have more management studies.

Philip was the first government-sponsored scholar to take up industrial engineering, and he had to explain to the Public Service Commission what the course was about when he switched to industrial engineering after his first year mechanical engineering study at the University of Toronto. His choice put him in good stead when he was appointed an Administrative Assistant and posted to Mindef in July 1970.

At Mindef, his training in industrial engineering proved invaluable when he was asked to set up from scratch a Systems Engineering branch in the Logistics Division. This entity was responsible for the analysis, research and design of more effective and efficient logistics operating systems, procedures and methods. Logistics is an American defence term for the systematic planning and provision of supply, transportation and maintenance of combat forces at all levels. 1970 was a critical year

Philip Yeo

for Mindef as Dr Goh Keng Swee took over as Minister of Defence and reorganized the total structure and systems of the Singapore Armed Forces. The demands on the logistics organization to purchase, supply and maintain a fast growing SAF were heavy and challenging.

Philip proved his mettle and was made Head of Organization and Control Department and Deputy Director of Logistics Division in May 1971. His ceaseless efforts saw the creation of the School of Logistics Administration in February 1973. In September that year, he was asked to cover the duties of the Director of Finance Division in Mindef. Here too, Philip brought to bear his flair for computer applications and data processing. He computerized the entire SAF payroll system and re-organized the defence budgeting system.

His dedicated and determined efforts did not go unnoticed: he was awarded the Public Administration (Silver) Medal and promoted to Assistant Secretary in 1974, and Principal Assistant Secretary in 1975.

Even while he was engrossed in his work, Philip still found time to keep up his studies on a part-time basis with the University of Singapore. This earned him his Masters in Systems Engineering in August 1974.

His management and academic performance won him a United States Department of State Fellowship to do his Masters in Business Administration at Harvard University in 1974. He was the first civil servant to enjoy this honour.

After successful completion of the course, Philip was made Director of Logistics Division in June 1976. He was also appointed executive director of Chartered Industries of Singapore and Ordnance Development and Engineering Company of Singapore, chairman of Singapore Automotive Engineering Ltd., and director of Allied Ordnance Company of Singapore. These are government-owned companies responsible for the production of arms and ammunition and the repair and overhaul of military vehicles and tanks. The four companies together employ nearly 3,000 workers.

Whilst managing these companies, he was also involved in introducing minicomputer systems for on-line logistics management in the SAF. Four minicomputers were installed over two years, from January 1977, in the general equipment, ordnance spares, ammunition and air force supply bases. He also introduced two minicomputers in Singapore Automotive Engineering and Chartered Industries.

He was promoted to Deputy Secretary Grade "G" in 1977 and in May 1978 was appointed First Deputy Secretary of Mindef. From August, he will be acting Second Permanent Secretary of the ministry.

Asked to comment on his career development, Philip said: "Frankly, I had not given any thought to it. I was so busy getting jobs done; there was hardly time to worry about promotion. I am very happy that I could put into practice what I had studied. I find fulfilment in my job. That's more important than anything else."

Pay revision for teachers

The salary scales of honours graduate teachers in the education service are now on par with those in the administrative service following a revision in the education service's salary structure.

The revisions, which will also benefit pass degree holders and others upon promotion, will cost the government $4.5 million a year in additional expenditure.

Singapore Bulletin July 1979.
Source: Philip Yeo

Top and bottom: The National Computer Board and the Defence Ministry are studying the possible use of artificial intelligence in computer-assisted instruction. This was revealed by Mindef's Second Permanent Secretary (Defence), Philip Yeo, when he opened five computer-assisted instruction centres at the School of Combat Engineers (SOCE) in Gillman Barracks on 19 August 1983. Artificial intelligence refers to the branch of computer science which seeks to make computers think like human beings. *Source: Singapore Press Holdings*

Philip Yeo examines the Kite, a new night aiming scope for weapons in 1987. With him is Robert O' Neill (Director, International Institute for Strategic Studies, London). *Source: Singapore Press Holdings*

Philip Yeo at the launching of RSS Valiant on 22 July 1989 by Minister of Defence BG (Res) Lee Hsien Loong. *Source: Ministry of Defence*

(Left to right) Lam Chuan Leong (Permanent Secretary, Ministry of Trade & Industry), Philip Yeo (Chairman, EDB), Peter Chan (Permanent Secretary, Ministry of Foreign Affairs) and Tan Chin Nam (Managing Director, EDB) at the Global Strategies-The Singapore Partnership conference in October 1988. *Source: Economic Development Board*

Philip Yeo at the establishment of Glaxo-IMCB Research Venture in 1989. *Source: Economic Development Board*

(Left to right) Teo Chee Hean (Minister of State, Ministry of Finance & Communications), S Jayakumar (Minister for Foreign Affairs), Goh Chok Tong (Prime Minister), Tan Boon Teik (former Attorney-General), Yeo Cheow Tong (Minister for Trade and Industry), Philip Yeo (Chairman, EDB) at the Singapore Forum 1994. *Source: Economic Development Board*

Philip Yeo (Chairman, EDB) stepping in to view an exhibition of Levi products yesterday in conjunction with a ceremony marking the award of Operational Headquarters (OHQ) status in the company on 2 September 1995. *Source: Singapore Press Holdings*

Illustrations of Philip Yeo taken from EDB – The Next Lap Cartoon booklet, 1991.
Artist: Lee Hup Kheng

(Left to right) Ko Kheng Hwa (CEO, JTC), Kwa Chong Seng (Chairman and Managing Director, Esso Singapore) and Philip Yeo (Chairman, EDB) looking at the model of Jurong Island during the launch of the partial road link to Jurong Island in 1999. At second left is Teo Ming Kian (Permanent Secretary, Ministry of Communications). *Source: Singapore Press Holdings*

(Left to right) Alfred Voskian (President and Managing Director, Eastman Chemical Asia Pacific), Philip Yeo (Chairman, EDB) and Earnest Deavenport Jr (Chairman and CEO, Eastman Chemical Company) having a chat in front of the newly inaugurated Eastman's Singapore Oxo Chemicals Complex on Jurong Island in 1999. *Source: Singapore Press Holdings*

Philip Yeo accompanying BG (Res) Lee Hsien Loong; Radius Prawiro (Coordinating Minister for Economy and Industry, Indonesia) and Tunky Ariwibowo (State Minister for Industry, Indonesia) on a visit to Bintan, Indonesia in 1991. *Source: Economic Development Board*

(Left to right) Peter F Gontha (co-founder, Chandra Asri), Philip Yeo (Chairman, EDB) and Tunky Ariwibowo (State Minister for Industry, Indonesia) worked closely on the implementation of the Singapore-Riaus Economic Cooperation Projects. *Source: Philip Yeo*

(Left to right) Philip Yeo with Barry Desker (Ambassador to Indonesia, Singapore), Radius Prawiro (Coordinating Minister of the Economics, Finance and Industry and Development Supervisory Board, Indonesia), S Dhanabalan (Minister of Trade and Industry, Singapore), Tunky Ariwibowo (State Minister for Industry, Indonesia). *Source: Philip Yeo*

(Left to right) Philip Yeo with Anthony Salim (President, Salim Group) and Wong Kok Siew (CEO, Sembcorp Industries) who were the Indonesia-Singapore partners for several Indonesia-Singapore Riaus Economic Cooperation projects. *Source: Philip Yeo*

REUTERS

Good friends: *Mr Yeo paying a courtesy call on President Habibie in Jakarta yesterday*

Indon firms will gain from Natuna pipeline: EDB chief

From **Shoeb Kagda**
in Jakarta

ECONOMIC Development Board (EDB) chairman Philip Yeo yesterday said Indonesian companies stand to gain from the development of the 470-kilometre pipeline linking the huge Natuna natural gas field to Singapore.

As most of the fabrication work for the pipeline will be done in Indonesia, there will be opportunities for Indonesian companies to provide raw materials and engineering expertise. "This is the first time for both Singapore and Indonesia to engage in such a major engineering project," he noted.

In Jakarta for a two-day visit, Mr Yeo told journalists after a one-hour meeting with President BJ Habibie that he is also exploring new economic projects with Indonesia and that the two countries continue to enjoy good economic relations.

"I conveyed my best wishes to President Habibie, who is a good friend and a big brother to me. I have worked very closely with him on the Batam Industrial Park for many years," said Mr Yeo. "I am here to see what we can do to help Indonesia on economic projects."

He added that there is no reason why economic confidence cannot return to Indonesia as the Batam Industrial Park is still attracting new investors. "When I go out to market the project, I market Indonesia and we are willing to assist Indonesia in any other way." On the Natuna gas pipeline project, Mr Yeo said eight international consortiums have submitted tenders and that a decision on the tender winner will be made by November. He added that the pipeline must be completed by the end of 2000, with shipments to start by April 2001.

Singapore has agreed to buy 325 million cu feet of natural gas a day from Indonesia under a payment guarantee scheme. The natural gas is to be used by power plants in the Republic.

Sticking to the timetable is very important to Singapore as it needs to decide whether to use natural gas or fuel oil to meet its energy demands for the future, Mr Yeo said.

The Business Times, 2 September 1998.
Source: Singapore Press Holdings

Philip Yeo (front row, third from left) with Executive Vice Premier Zhu Rongji (front row, centre) and members of the Singapore official delegation, Ho Ching (front row, second from right), Seah Kia Ger (front row, first from left), Liew Mun Leong (second row, second from left), Wong Kok Siew (second row, third from right), David Lim (back row, first from left) and Lim Swee Say (back row, second from left) in 1993. *Source: Philip Yeo*

Launch of Singapore-Suzhou Club: (from right) DPM BG Lee, Suzhou party secretary Chen Deming and Philip Yeo. *Source: Singapore Press Holdings*

Philip Yeo leading the Singapore delegation during the Japan Association Corporation Executives, Keidanren mission to China-Singapore Suzhou Industrial Park in 1996. *Source: Suzhou Industrial Park Administrative Committee (SIPAC) / China-Singapore Suzhou Industrial Park Development Group Co Ltd. (CSSD)*

Lim Swee Say (MD, EDB and Director, Singapore Software Projects Office) with Singapore businessmen and Chinese officials at Suzhou Industrial Park during Prime Minister Goh Chok Tong's visit in 1997. *Source: Singapore Press Holdings*

(Seated, left to right) EDB chairman Philip Yeo, Singapore High Commissioner to India Wong Kwok Pun and Tata Industries chairman Ratan Tata in a good mood after signing up 19 new investors in the International Tech Park at Whitefield near Bangalore. *Source: Singapore Press Holdings*

A visit to the International Technology Park in Bangalore by the Board of Ascendas Property Fund Trust (APFT) on 20 March 2009. This photo was taken at the then newly opened International Airport at Bangalore. (From left) David Lim (Chairman, Investment Committee), Sundaresh Menon (board member), Lim Hock San (Chairman, Audit Committee), Philip Yeo (Chairman, APFT), Siak Ching (CEO, Ascendas Singapore), Jonathan Yap (CEO, AiTrust), Amal Ganguli (board member). *Source: David Lim*

Philip Yeo (Chairman, EDB) witnesses the signing ceremony for 11 companies to get licences to operate in Vietnam-Singapore Industrial Park (VSIP). (Centre between flags) VSIP Executive Chairman Lai Chun Loong and (right) VSIP Vice-chairman Nguyen Van Hung officiate the signing ceremony. *Source: Singapore Press Holdings*

Sembcorp Development's seventh Vietnam-Singapore Industrial Park (VSIP). The project, which is in Nghe An province, about 400km from Hanoi and 70km from the Laos border, is being developed by a partnership between Vietnam's Becamex IDC Corporation, which has a 49 per cent stake in the joint venture, and a Singapore consortium – in which Sembcorp has a 92.9 per cent stake. *Source: Sembcorp Industries Ltd*

WHO WOULD BE MAD ENOUGH TO INVEST IN SINGAPORE IN A RECESSION?

"WE ARE"

John Sculley

JOHN SCULLEY, CHAIRMAN & CEO
APPLE COMPUTER, INC.

"WE ARE AS WELL"

Edson D. de Castro

EDSON D. DE CASTRO, PRESIDENT
DATA GENERAL CORP.

"WE ARE TOO"

Robert W. Galvin

ROBERT W. GALVIN, CHAIRMAN
MOTOROLA, INC.

"SO ARE WE"

Charles E. Sporck

CHARLES E. SPORCK, PRESIDENT & CEO
NATIONAL SEMICONDUCTOR CORP.

"WE ARE"

Joe M. Henson

JOE M. HENSON, PRESIDENT & CEO
PRIME COMPUTER, INC.

"WE ARE AS WELL"

Alan F. Shugart

ALAN F. SHUGART, CHAIRMAN & CEO
SEAGATE TECHNOLOGY INC.

"WE ARE"

Carmelo J. Santoro

CARMELO J. SANTORO, CHAIRMAN & CEO
SILICON SYSTEMS INC.

"WE ARE TOO"

Evans W. Erikson

EVANS W. ERIKSON, CHAIRMAN & CEO
SUNDSTRAND CORP.

"SO ARE WE"

Harry J. Gray

HARRY J. GRAY, CHAIRMAN
UNITED TECHNOLOGIES CORP.

Singapore's growth rate over the last twenty years has been a phenomenal 9% per annum.

Until last year.

When it registered what economists tend to euphemistically refer to as 'negative growth.'

Why on earth then, are some of America's sanest and most successful companies either expanding their operations or moving into the country for the first time?

Could it be that in an analysis by the US Department of Commerce, Singapore shows one of the highest returns on investment for American companies abroad?

Maybe it's Singapore's location in South East Asia? A potential market of some 270 million people.

Or its sophisticated telecommunications network, its eight-hour port turnaround, and one of the most efficient airports in the world, all of which make it the perfect regional headquarters.

Possibly its people? Multi-racial and proficient in many languages, including English and Mandarin, an asset when doing business in China.

Or its democratic government?

With its strong commitment to competitiveness and free enterprise. Typified recently by major cuts in personal and corporate taxes and a series of new investment incentives.

And its unparalleled 25-year track record of political stability. For where else would substantial overnight wage cost reductions win the agreement and full support of unions and workers?

Or is it simply that US investors realise the current recession is merely a hiccup?

There seems to be method in their madness.

SINGAPORE
THE BUSINESS CENTER OF ASIA

FOR MORE INFORMATION, PLEASE CONTACT YOUR NEAREST SINGAPORE ECONOMIC DEVELOPMENT BOARD CENTER: NEW YORK, TEL: (212) 421-2200. ATLANTA, TEL: (404) 939-8600. BOSTON, TEL: (617) 577-0190. CHICAGO, TEL: (312) 644-1730. DALLAS, TEL: (214) 450-4540. LOS ANGELES, TEL: (213) 624-3591. NEW CANAAN (CONNECTICUT), TEL: (203) 966-6504. SAN FRANCISCO, TEL: (415) 981-9800. WASHINGTON DC, TEL: (202) 223-2571. OR OUR HEADQUARTERS IN SINGAPORE, TEL: 271-0844.

Source: Economic Development Board

WHO WOULD BE MAD ENOUGH TO WORK FOR PHILIP YEO?

"I AM"

TAN CHIN NAM
CHAIRMAN
MDA

"I AM AS WELL"

DAVID LIM
SENIOR ADVISOR
HEXAGON DEVELOPMENT ADVISORS

"ME ALSO"

LIM SWEE SAY
SG
NTUC

"SO AM I"

BEH SWAN GIN
MD
EDB

"I AM TOO"

CHONG LIT CHEONG
CEO
IE

"I AM "

TEO ENG CHEONG
CEO-DESIGNATE
IE

"I AM AS WELL "

MANOHAR KHIATANI
CEO
JTC

"SO AM I"

LEE YI SHYAN
MOS
MTI

"I AM TOO"

KOH LIN-NET
DS
MTI

"I AM "

JOSEPHINE YONG
ASST SG
NTUC

"I AM AS WELL"

PNG CHEONG BOON
CEO
SPRING

"YES, I AM"

AW KAH PENG
CEO
STB

"ME TOO"

KHOO SEOK LIN
TRAINER
& FACILITATOR

Philip Yeo has been described by Harvard Business School as an "overseer of Singapore's economic direction" with "so much to do" that he "sets a very fast pace". Indeed. Those who work with him know that notes of meetings are to be submitted within 24 hours, and follow-up actions taken within the next 24 hours. He eschews political correctness and diplomatic politeness. He is direct and straight talking. He can liberally stamp "BS!!!" in red ink when he disagrees with views expressed in papers sent to him. An officer is allowed to make mistakes — 3 a year, to be exact — but not the same ones as that would indicate that you have learnt NOTHING. Mistakes are accepted because they are the best source of learning. It is a quota that is quite easily used up given the complex projects and issues he gives to young officers. Throwing them into the deep end of the pool is one of his methods of inducting promising young officers.

Why on earth then do some of Singapore's most successful leaders in public service want to work for and with him, and continue to do so long after their official service with him is over?

Could it be that they learnt all about passion and commitment from this man who epitomises these values? To always wholeheartedly believe in, enjoy and have fun with what we are doing at work? Or move on.

Maybe it is because they all flourished under his "fly a kite" (let- go- and -rein -in) brand of people development — letting each soar on their passion and capabilities yet setting boundaries where necessary?

Or is it because they admire his principle-centred and purpose-anchored philosophy of making decisions based on what is right and what serves the national interest, and not on what is convenient or popular? Even when these actions bring showers of harsh criticism. They learn what true courage, integrity and taking risks really mean.

Possibly it is because he shows genuine care and concern for his people? From simple things like making sure they have a good meal after a hectic day of running around with him on overseas trips. To meeting up his scholars in each city he visits to encourage, advise, counsel and feed them. To asking after their families, especially the kids (and when they grew up — to offer advice on college, jobs, graduate schools…). In his own unique way, he gives personal attention to the development of his people. In so doing, he has helped hundreds of ordinary officers realize their potential and achieve extra-ordinary things.

Perhaps it is his unending curiosity and passion for new knowledge that infects everyone around him? The countless articles of every conceivable topic under the sun that he sends to everyone, or in today's world, where he "dropbox"es into everyone's virtual in-tray, to remind us all to learn, to grow, to always have a sense of wonder and keep a wider perspective of the world.

Philip Yeo lives out the Tagore quote "Work is Love Made Visible". He teaches us by his example to love the work we do, to offer our best gifts and talents to the work, and to care for the people we do the work with and for. How else can he himself and those who work with him sustainably put in the 12 to 18-hour work days…the frequent travels away from home to seek opportunities for Singapore and its people… oftentimes through weekends and holidays?

Or is it simply that his leadership and mentorship enabled each to be more like him — a M.A.D. C.O.W. (Making a Difference, Changing Our World)?

There seems to be a method to his and their madness.

PHILIP YEO
THE PEOPLE AND TALENT DEVELOPER.

Source: Philip Yeo

BG (NS) George Yeo at the groundbreaking of Biopolis, with MG (NS) Lim Neo Chian (Chairman, JTC) and Philip Yeo. *Source: Singapore Press Holdings*

Opening of Biopolis Phase II: (Left to right) Thomas Teo (CEO, Ascendas Land (S) Pte Ltd), Lew Syn Pau (Chairman, Ascendas Pte Ltd), Philip Yeo (Chairman, A*STAR), Colin Blakemore (CEO, UK Medical Research Council) and Philip Su (Assistant CEO, JTC).
Source: Ascendas-Singbridge Pte Ltd

(Left to right) Philip Yeo, Paul Marks (President and CEO, Memorial Sloan Kettering Cancer Center), Keith Peters (Regius Professor of Physic, University of Cambridge), Axel Ullrich (Director of the Department of Molecular Biology, Max-Planck-Institute of Biochemistry in Martinsried), Sydney Brenner (Founder, Molecular Sciences Institute in Berkeley, California USA) and Richard Sykes (Rector, Imperial College London) – Men who have made their mark in life sciences. *Source: Singapore Press Holdings*

Exterior of Fusionopolis. The Singapore's major research hub for the science, engineering, infocommunication and media industries is decked with sky gardens, restaurants, a fitness centre and even a theatre. *Source: JTC Corporation*

The 2001–2002 yearbook for A*STAR, which features this sketch of A*STAR chairman Philip Yeo, is peppered with space analogies. *Source: Agency for Science, Technology and Research (A*STAR)*

A*STAR scholarship advertisement featuring a DNA tattoo.
Source: Agency for Science, Technology and Research (A*STAR)

Philip Yeo (Chairman, A*STAR) receives a gift from S R Nathan (President, Singapore) after the latter unveiled the artwork "Biopolis" (background) at the Matrix Building. On the left is Lim Hng Kiang (Minister for Trade and Industry, Singapore). The seven panels of the artwork designed by Associate Professor David S Goodsell of Scripps Research Institute in the US are an exploration of cell, the molecular basis of life. *Source: Singapore Press Holdings*

International advisory council for biomedical sciences to announce new initiatives for A*STAR. (Left to right) Richard Sykes (Rector, Imperial College London), Philip Yeo (Chairman, A*STAR) and LG (NS) Lim Chuan Poh. *Source: Singapore Press Holdings*

Year 2000: (Left to right) Tan Chorh Chuan (Chairman, NUH Medical Board), John Wong (Head Department of Medical Oncology, NUS), Kong Hwai Loong (Associate Professor of Medicine, NUS) and Philip Yeo. *Source: Singapore Press Holdings*

Year 2016: (Left to right) Tan Chorh Chuan (President, NUS), Kong Hwai Loong (Senior Consultant Medical Oncologist and Physician, Mount Elizabeth Medical Centre and Novena Medical Center), Sydney Brenner (Senior Fellow, A*STAR) and Philip Yeo. *Source: Philip Yeo*

Top and bottom: The biomedical sciences pioneers then and now.

Philip Yeo at the launch of the Marine and Offshore Technology Centres of Innovation funded under SPRING's S$150 million Technology Innovation Programme in 2008. *Source: Standards, Productivity and Innovation Board Singapore (SPRING)*

Philip Yeo with the recipients of SPRING Singapore's Executive Development Scholarships in 2010. *Source: Standards, Productivity and Innovation Board Singapore (SPRING)*

Philip Yeo (Chairman, EDB) gesticulates while talking to some of the new scholars during the Glaxo Wellcome-EDB Scholarship Award Ceremony at Westin Stamford Hotel in 1998. The scholars will be studying in universities in US, UK, Canada, Japan and Singapore. The four scholars from left: Eugenie Lam Chi Li, Pang Kah Ling, Raymond Han Yew Hong, Urmi Gupta. *Source: Singapore Press Holdings*

---

14 home

thesundaytimes July 28, 2013

Award to spread the 'Philip Yeo passion'

WHO WOULD BE MAD ENOUGH TO WANT TO CHANGE OUR WORLD?

ST PHOTO: KEVIN LIM

Spring Singapore chairman Philip Yeo was honoured at a dinner on Friday attended by National University of Singapore staff, students and many of the people he has mentored.

NUS scholarship named after Spring Singapore chairman aims to foster entrepreneurship

Chang Ai-Lien
Senior Correspondent

Mr Philip Yeo recounts an occasion when he and Mr Lim Swee Say – then working with him at the Economic Development Board – were queueing up for their boarding passes at an airline transit counter in Chicago.

As there would be no food on the plane, he asked the young officer accompanying them to get three hot dogs from the nearest food stand.

"Swee Say and I got our boarding passes in less than 15 minutes, then we went looking for our missing officer," said Mr Yeo.

"We found him at the hot dog stand – patiently putting ketchup, onions, condiments, et cetera, et cetera onto the three hot dogs! I expected him to bring the three 'naked' hot dogs to us. The officer failed the hot dog test. No more future trips with us."

Those who have worked under the man know this is a Philip Yeo classic.

Known to talk and walk a mile a minute, he has little patience for those who cannot keep up. But the 67-year-old is also known for his passion for those working with him, and for Singapore. In a varied 43-year career in the public sector, he has brought in billions of dollars of investments, conjured up industries practically from thin air, and created thousands of jobs.

At a dinner on Friday attended by National University of Singapore staff, students and many of the people he has mentored, the

Spring Singapore chairman was honoured with an NUS scholarship named after him, in the hope that some of his magic will rub off on more young folk.

"His brand of leadership is unique," said former Ascendas chief Chong Siak Ching. "He dares to push boundaries and to do what's right, not for himself, but for the nation."

Minister in the Prime Minister's Office Lim Swee Say, who was present, said: "I learnt from him some very important values: never say die, always dare to be different, always want to make a difference. We cannot duplicate Philip Yeo, but the least we can do is to spread this Philip Yeo spirit, this Philip Yeo culture, and most importantly the Philip Yeo passion."

Ms Chong, now chief executive officer of The National Art Gallery,

Singapore, has rounded up other enthusiastic members of a fund-raising and selection committee who have benefited from working with Mr Yeo. They call themselves "Mad Cows" after his brand of leadership which is all about "making a difference, changing our world".

About $2 million has been raised for the scholarship endowment fund so far, which, with the Government matching, will mean a $5 million fund that will send about 10 recipients abroad each year. More donors are expected to grow the fund.

Recipients will get stints at top universities and work experience at start-ups and companies.

They will also get to meet Mr Yeo and some of his vast network of friends and contacts worldwide, said NUS president Tan Chorh Chuan. "He has a very genuine in-

terest in helping young people and he continues to be your mentor; it's a long-term relationship, which explains why there's such a network of goodwill for him."

NUS has an existing scholarship scheme where students study and work abroad for a year in places ranging from Silicon Valley and Israel to Beijing and Bangalore, and the best of the best will be chosen for the "Philip Yeo Initiative", said Dr Lily Chan, head of the university's innovation and entrepreneurship promotion arm, NUS Enterprise.

She noted that, already, one in five students on such stints ends up starting his own company. "When they come back, they think differently," she said. "And if they start a business in the style and spirit of Philip Yeo, they will dare to do anything."

Mr Yeo told The Sunday Times: "My job is almost like a sifu (master). I will interact with them and give them advice, and Spring can potentially help fund them with seed capital.

"To get the best out of people, don't be paternalistic. You have to treat them like kites," he said. "You get them up in the air, if there's no wind you tug again. Everybody needs a lift-off. If they get into trouble, you reel them in."

allien@sph.com.sg

Chance to study, work abroad... and network too

The Philip Yeo Initiative will give National University of Singapore students and graduates an opportunity to study and work abroad as well as personal time with Mr Yeo and his network of contacts.

It comprises two scholarships – a

full-time programme which is an offshoot of the university's 10-year-old entrepreneurship effort called NUS Overseas College; and a part-time one available to both students and alumni.

From next year, around five stu-

dents from the first programme – called the Philip Yeo Entrepreneurial Awards – will be funded to spend up to a year abroad, working and studying in leading entrepreneurial hubs all over the world.

In the second scheme – the

Philip Yeo Innovation Fellows – another five recipients will visit major entrepreneurial hubs overseas and meet leaders in their respective fields to further their ideas under customised programmes.

Chang Ai-Lien

Straits Times report on the launch of the Philip Yeo Initiative (PYI), 28 July 2013.
Source: Singapore Press Holdings

Philip Yeo with potential candidates for the PYI Innovation Fellowship Award at the launch, 28 July 2013. *Source: Philip Yeo Initiative (PYI)*

Trio win Philip Yeo Initiative scholarships

Beyond funding, programme opens doors, offers valuable mentorship

By LINETTE LAI

UNDERGRADUATE Kenneth Lou was fed up with having to use chunky portable phone chargers, so he designed his own.

The result: a sleek, wireless charging case that takes Mr Lou a step closer to his dream of a wireless world.

Besides raising nearly $120,000 on Kickstarter, the 23-year-old's vision also caught the attention of those behind the Philip Yeo Initiative.

Mr Lou is now one of the first three to be picked as an associate with the Initiative. This means access to a programme that provides funding, mentorship and networking opportunities.

First launched in 2013 with an initial backing of $5 million, the Philip Yeo Initiative recently raised more than half a million through a golf and dinner event.

With matching government grants, the fund is expected to total around $6 million.

The programme offers two types of scholarships.

The first – an offshoot of the National University of Singapore's Overseas Colleges programme – gives 10 students the opportunity to spend up to a year studying and working in entrepreneurial hubs all over the world.

The second, which Mr Lou is part of, grants winners up to $20,000 in funding to realise their projects.

The other two winners are 28-year-old Fitzkhoon Liang, who studied engineering science, and 29-year-old Jan Lim, who studied architecture.

Participants said the value of the programme is in the doors it opens and the experience its mentors bring to the table.

Mr Lou recalled how the idea for his product won many business plan competitions, but got off to a slow start until his mentor gave him a wake-up call.

"He asked me, do you want to win business plan awards forever? Or do you want to start a company?" said Mr Lou.

For Ms Lim, whose project is about helping communities play a

bigger part in shaping their environment, the game-changer was taking two trips to New York and Copenhagen.

"That was quite a pivotal moment – speaking to the people in the design industry," she said.

But while the mentors provide support and guidance, they do not spoon-feed their young charges.

"There's no guarantee that if you join this programme you won't fail," said Mr Liang, who is trying to develop a universal handyman service to meet seniors' housekeeping needs.

"In February, my company crashed. I was shell-shocked. But my mentors weren't. They just said pick yourself up and go at it again."

Those behind the recent fund-raising effort, such as Ms Chong Siak Ching, said that the programme is about opening doors for those with a clear goal and the passion to achieve it.

"It is not for us to tell them what to do," she said. "It is for them to tell us what they need to succeed."

✉ linette@sph.com.sg

(From left) Mr Kenneth Lou, Mr Fitzkhoon Liang and Ms Jan Lim won scholarships from the Philip Yeo Initiative, which offers funding, mentorship, and networking opportunities. PHOTO: LIM YAOHUI FOR THE STRAITS TIMES

Pioneer PYI Innovation Associates (left to right) Kenneth Lou (Novelsys), Fitzkhoon Liang (AfterYou), Jan Lim (Participate in Design). *Source: Singapore Press Holdings*

Interview sessions with
Philip Yeo for this book.

Bottom: **Author Peh Shing
Huei (in blue) and Han
Fook Kwang (centre) in
Philip Yeo's office.** *Source:
Singapore Press Holdings
Photographer: Lim Yaohui*

My Chemical Romance

"This is the first time I have ever bought a building site that is under water."

An unidentified board member of Eastman Chemical Company, when
approving his firm's plan for a plant on Jurong Island, from
The Making of Jurong Island: The Right Chemistry.

Lucio Noto settled onto a couch in a private room at the Raffles Hotel and lit a cigar. The bald American with a thick moustache drew in the smoke. He held it in his mouth, savouring the flavour. The Hawaiian shirt on his thick frame could not mask the rough cut of a man brought up by Sicilian immigrant parents in a rough Brooklyn neighbourhood. He paused. The man who rose through the ranks to head oil giant Mobil was in no hurry and he was waiting for the courtship from his three Singaporean visitors to begin. One of them popped the question: Would Mobil consider investing in a Singapore island which did not exist? Noto exhaled and blew the smoke into the face of Philip Yeo. The EDB chairman did not flinch. "It was akin to convincing a Mafia boss," said Yeoh Keat Chuan, who was part of the Singapore trio.

Noto, brought up by a unionist Italian father, steeped in the cutthroat world of the New York labour movement, was a skilled negotiator. He challenged Yeo and his team: "Give me 10 reasons why I should invest in Singapore." In typical exuberant Philip Yeo fashion, he and his team gave 11. The list included Singapore's stable and pro-business investment environment; a skilled workforce and how Jurong Island would help Mobil integrate their existing refinery and aromatics operations. Noto listened intently and Yeo sensed a deal could be sealed. As Yeoh, who is now managing director of EDB, recalled: "Noto seemed to be the type of leader who would commit to something once he gave his word." But the Mobil chairman and CEO was getting angsty. There was no ashtray in the room. Yeoh stepped out, approached the hotel staff but was told it was a "no smoking" room. He slinked his way to the famous Long Bar, "borrowed" an ashtray and stuffed it into his pocket. The effort paid off. Noto said yes. Mobil, which later became ExxonMobil, signed on to build the US$2 billion Singapore Chemical Complex in 1997. It was the world's fourth-largest petrochemical cracker. It was the single biggest investment in the history of Singapore.

130

Jurong Island is the single biggest feat in Philip Yeo's career. Its audacity remains stunning more than two decades later. The project merged seven islands into one through reclamation. It sold land which did not exist. It lured investors with an imaginary product, promising utilities, drainage and roads when the only thing visible was the sea. As then-Prime Minister Goh Chok Tong said at its official opening in 2000: "Selling stretches of seawater, with only the promise of land sometime in the future, must surely be more difficult than selling ice cream to the Eskimos!" In short, they had to be sold a dream. And Yeo was the best salesman of this fantasy on the sea.

The origins of Jurong Island are a little murkier than the clear shallow waters which it sits on. Both Jurong Town Corporation (JTC) and EDB have competing claims to its genesis. JTC said it came up with the idea of joining up all the Southern islands off Jurong in the 1980s. Credit, according to the organisation, goes to its head of civil and structural engineering department Ong Geok Soo, who doodled the shape of the giant island on paper. "By the late 1980s, JTC had completed the concept plan for the amalgamation of the islands – a tremendous undertaking that would create an island twice the size of the Ang Mo Kio HDB estate and almost that of the Jurong industrial estate," according to *The Making of Jurong Island*, a book by JTC. It started enlarging some of the islands, although they remained distinct and were not connected.

EDB has a slightly different take. It said that while JTC had the idea, "the prevailing view was that the southern islands were a 'long-term' development, for which there was no immediate use," wrote officers Gong Wee Lik and Tan Suan Swee – two key players behind the project – in *Heartwork*, a book by EDB. They added: "Not much was done beyond piecemeal reclamation. 131 Because they were offshore, these islands were considered the backwaters, such that typically the most junior JTC officer was assigned to oversee them." The origins of the project, according to EDB, came from a flight by Yeo in the early 1990s. He was on a helicopter ride back to Singapore after scouring Indonesia's Karimun islands for a shipyard site. He flew by the seven small islands and the tide was just going out in the evening.

"My guests were pointing out how shallow the channels between the islands were and that silting could cause a problem for bunkering," Yeo wrote in *Heartwork*. He asked the pilot to fly lower and closer to those waters. The pilot kept saying it was dangerous as they were flying over oil refineries. The chopper got close enough for Yeo to like what he saw. He recalled: "It sounded like a crazy idea, but what if we filled up the channels to link up the seven islands and create a big one? An offshore island, where petrochemical complexes could be built sounded like a good idea. We touched down in Singapore and I called up my guys when I reached back to the office."

While the origins of the formation of Jurong Island may be contested, it is indisputable that the idea that it should host a self-contained petrochemical hub belongs to Yeo and EDB. JTC chairman Lim Neo Chian said: "You can have an island of 3,000 hectares, but you can do many things, right? It can be just an extension of Jurong industrial park where you can put all kinds of factories there. Or it could be something different, which is what EDB did. EDB conceived the idea of a petrochemical hub on Jurong Island being detached from the mainland." It was the coming together of "two powerful ideas", he added. One, merging the seven islands into one. Two, marketing the island as a petrochemical hub. "Rather than market to any Tom, Dick or Harry, to any company, Singapore wanted a petrochemical hub, 3,000,000–4,000,000 tonnes of ethylene a year, with common facilities that will serve all the different companies. That gives the petrochemical companies a reason to look at it seriously." As then-Deputy Prime Minister Lee Hsien Loong said in 2000 when he opened the bridge linking the island to the mainland: "Full credit must go to EDB for the success of Jurong Island. Together with JTC and the many government agencies involved in the project, they have taken the lead in conceiving and promoting Jurong Island, and continually planning ahead to take it on to the next stage of success."

Yeo's idea was to build what he called the "Sim Lim Square of petrochemicals", referring to the popular electronics mall in Singapore. Everything will be housed under one roof, or on one island in this case. More importantly, the products of one company will feed off one another. The technical term is "vertical integration". What it means is for the output of one plant to become the input of another. Oil refineries, for example, will produce raw petrochemical materials which are fed downstream to players like Sumitomo and DuPont to make paints, textiles and synthetic leather. One company's supplier is the other's customer, said Yeo. To use an analogy, it is akin to having the chicken farm, the egg seller and an omelette shop next to one another.

The companies will also share utilities by outsourcing common facilities, such as cooling water, waste treatment and steam to third-party specialists like Sembcorp and Power Seraya. This helps the firms enjoy economies of scale and lower costs. And by cutting down the capital costs of building jetties, tanks and pipelines, Jurong Island is a good 20 per cent cheaper option for a petrochemical firm to get its plant running. That is not all. By being so close to Singapore's mega port, these companies can easily send their products overseas. "I found no other hub like Singapore," said Singapore Petroleum Company's CEO Ng Cheng Cheong in *The Making*. "So compact, so close to a mega port that it takes minimum time to transit from factory to marketplace." In the words of JTC CEO Ko Kheng Hwa, Jurong Island offers companies a "plug and play" option in a multi-billion industry. "They build their plants, plug in, and start to produce," he said.

The idea was borne out of necessity. Singapore was looking to diversify its manufacturing base and the oil refining sector was facing strong competition. Countries were building their own refineries, reducing their demand for Singapore's exports. Yeo and his EDB team decided to promote chemicals aggressively. It was a much sought after one. The value add per worker is almost S$700,000 a year, eight times that of the manufacturing industry. And the world was already deep in the age of plastic. "The whole

133

world was becoming more and more dependent on plastic," Yeo said. "Tell me, in a car, how many things are made of wood today? There's no more wood. The good old dashboard is all plastic today. The seat is plastic, so are the cushions. Your motorcar tyres? It's not rubber. It's synthetic rubber made up of butylene, a petroleum byproduct."

But it was not useful to simply bring in a petrochemical company or two, like what Singapore used to do with the likes of Mobil and Esso. Yeo wanted a cluster, a "Christmas tree" of companies, from high end to low end. "If you create the cluster, you must make sure that they (the companies) service as well as support one another. We created a cluster because that was the only way for us to compete," he said. "We had no land, no domestic market, no oil," he added. "Our labour costs were higher compared to our neighbours and so were our land costs. These were all our handicaps. We had nothing. So the only way for us to be competitive was to bring in raw materials, treat the companies as a cluster, give maximum value add and then go down the chain." An example is Chevron Oronite, which located its Asia Pacific headquarters on Jurong Island. Its plant needed more than 40 different types of raw materials, such as purified carbon dioxide and caustic soda, and were able to get more than half of these within the island or the region. Said Yeo: "My idea of having an island away from the population, to be self-contained, fully downstream all the way, is unique. I was certain it would succeed. I'm not a gambler."

Alas, for quite a number of years, the world didn't quite agree. As he cryptically noted in *The Making*: "Nobody wanted us." Part of the problem was that EDB was very selective. It wanted only the best petrochemical corporations in the world, the market leaders. But such big players, like

Mobil's Noto, were not easily persuaded by a non-existent island. "Companies could not see the land itself, much less the tangible cost savings of integration and outsourcing which were the basis for the amalgamation," wrote Gong and Tan. "All that was on paper. Not many were convinced." The board persisted with the courtship of the big hitters. EDB went through what it called "the scary years" between 1992 and 1995. For three years, it drew just three investors. Meanwhile, the government approved a S$7 billion budget to create the island. Reclamation started in 1995. Tenants were scarce. "For some of these big international companies, it was literally the future of their companies at stake," said current EDB chairman Beh Swan Gin.

Yeo sent every overseas EDB officer to work. But he took the lead to sell, literally, the promised land. Top corporate honchos of the major chemical companies said to him: "Philip, you're asking me to do something very strange, but I will believe you this time." Indeed, for those three scary years, the Singaporeans sold on a "trust us" platform. Yeo hustled the companies so often that they said: "Oh, you are here again." The EDB officers refused to take no for an answer. Gong and Tan wrote: "We knocked on the doors of all major chemical companies. We sold them our strategies for the development of Jurong Island and, to pre-empt their 'oh, you're here again' response, we gave them updates on the progress of the project as we went along."

For a man who had built an industrial park in Batam in 16 months and who dismissed weapons development of machine guns, mortars and artillery as "easy", it says something about the magnitude of Jurong Island that he called it a "tough job". "You got to call all the companies one by one," he said. "There's also a cumulative effect. Once I break one or two key guys, I could run to the others and say, hey, I got your feedstock. You've got to run to and fro. You cannot sit down and wait for the manna from heaven. We had to chase every project. There's nothing more humiliating than when you have to sell. You must have supreme confidence in what you're trying to do, otherwise why should they believe in you? You must really believe in what you're going to do." This "many-to-many matchmaker" role, as described by Ko, was incredibly tedious.

A big player which got away was General Electric (GE), whose GE Plastic business was courted by Singapore for Jurong Island. But it remains a story much loved by the EDB mafia and Yeo. A team from Singapore had made the visit to GE's headquarters in New York and were received by Jack Welch, the chairman and CEO of the conglomerate. "He didn't send his *calefare*," recalled EDB officer Jonathan Kua, using a Singaporean slang for extras on a movie set. But the importance which Welch placed on the meeting was mismatched by the powerpoint presentation put up by Kua. The photo that he showed of Jurong Island was blurred. "It was fine when I prepared it the night before. Now, in front of Jack Welch, it looked like Jurong Island with haze. I was horrified," he recalled. But Yeo, without missing a beat, said it was "Jurong Island on a cloudy day". And for good measure, added: "I'm going to dock his bonus by a month." Welch laughed.

The horror show for Kua didn't end there. When he showed a slide of the major chemical companies, GE's logo was small and placed below its arch rival United Technologies Corporation. Yeo quickly chimed in: "Another month's bonus gone." Welch laughed again. Yeo remembered: "In the bloody presentation, Jonathan make four mistakes. Each mistake he made, I said 'one month gone'." Kua concurred. "By the end of the presentation, I was four months down. Amazingly, I wasn't offended or worried. Maybe I was just trying to survive the presentation," he said with a laugh. When it was over, Yeo asked Welch if he was satisfied with the presentation and if he should "return" Kua his bonus. Welch said okay and Yeo said: "Restored." Kua, who is now group director of industry development at A*STAR, lived to work another day. He said: "It was actually a good meeting, albeit at my expense. I saw how Chairman engaged Welch at the highest level. I felt quite foolish about the errors but nobody was interested in scolding me after that. That's how we learnt at EDB. We win a lot but not all the time. And Jurong Island was a tough one."

The breakthrough came in 1995. Celanese Chemicals, the world's top producer of vinyl acetate monomer, inked a deal to build a US$100 million plant on Jurong Island. It was scouting for a place in Asia to consolidate its market share in this region and was impressed enough to take the plunge. The company became EDB's calling card, which it used to lure other big players in. One by one, from the United States, Europe and Japan, they signed up: Mitsui, Eastman, Lonza, Teijin, Exxon, Denka, Asahi and Chevron. Even the Asian financial crisis in 1997 did not slow the growth of Jurong Island. While the region quaked against the backdrop of the recession, there was either a plant opening or a groundbreaking every month on the island. By the official opening in 2000, there were 60 leading petrochemical and related companies on the island, investing more than S$20 billion. The fantasy was realised and as Ko said in an interview with *The Straits Times* in 2000: "Philip is Jurong Island's No. 1 evangelist."

Q   *How did you get the idea of a petrochemical island?*

A   After our push for semiconductors, I was worried about what Singapore could do next. What else could we do? What other cluster can we set up? I spent a lot of time on the road, visiting companies with my officers. I took the opportunity to talk to people to find out what could be next. So part of my advantage was that I was talking to companies and learning what they wanted. The key for EDB is not to do masterplanning. It's to go out there and find out what the market wants.

So I learnt about chemicals and the importance of building a cluster. At the upstream you have Mobil, Exxon and Shell. And downstream, you have the chemical companies. They want to be together, in an area where everybody is. That creates a critical mass. You realise even in the retail sector, they go by clusters. If you have only one little shop, nobody will come. But when all the same type of shops are in one place, it will create a critical mass. Like Sim Lim Square. It looks ridiculous, but it works. Consumers like to go to a place where all the options are available, with lots of varieties for them to pick and choose. There's logic to it.[29]

I visited the petrochemical clusters in Rotterdam and Houston and, over time, people live there. Chemical projects are never permanently safe. All it needs is an accident. When you have housing around, it's quite dangerous. So when I was thinking of a petrochemical cluster, I wanted it on an island and I didn't want anybody to live on that island. The island should just be for production because I don't want to risk the lives of people by having homes there. So every morning, people go into the island to work and in the evening, they leave. That's it. If there's a fire or accident, we could contain it more easily. It's safer. The only people who live

---

29   Business studies refer to this as "retail agglomeration". It is based on a "theory of cumulative attraction", which believes that consumers do not have perfect information and like to compare prices and products. In this way, the cluster will draw more customers, benefiting all the shops even though they are rivals.

on the island are those from the fire brigade, who have their own fire station.[30]

Q *Were the seven Southern Islands your first choice?*

A No, my first choice was Sentosa! I wanted a self-contained island and the best location was Sentosa. It's an island by itself. Nobody lives there.

Q *But it was already earmarked for tourism.*

A Oh, there was nothing. Before the casino came in, there was nothing. Only a few people went there every weekend. I know Sentosa because when I was at Mindef, the combat engineers were based there.[31] It was called Pulau Belakang Mati then and there was nothing there. But the government said no to my idea of turning it into a chemical island. Anyway, it's too small. It's only about 340 hectares. I needed 3,000 hectares. So we dropped the idea.

A lot of people have forgotten that Singapore was looking to develop the islands since the 1970s through reclamation. When I was in Mindef, we reclaimed Pulau Tekong and enlarged it significantly. Tekong was not the size it is today. Just like with the chemical plants, I wanted to move the army away from the mainland. That's how our camps started appearing on Tekong.[32]

Q *Back to Jurong Island. How difficult was it to sell to the major companies?*

---

30 A huge fire broke out on Jurong Island in April 2016, after an oil tank caught fire. It took five hours to put out the fire. No one was hurt.

31 The SAF combat engineers were based in Sentosa in the 1970s, taking over the barracks vacated by the British army.

32 Pulau Tekong was Singapore's largest island until the appearance of Jurong Island. In 1976, reclamation work started to expand its 1,700 hectares. Today, it is about 2,400 hectares and is used largely for military training.

A   Well, first and foremost, they couldn't see the land. They saw only the sea. The land was being reclaimed. I remember the chairman and CEO of Teijin, Mr Hiroshi Itagaki, being sceptical because such reclamation projects in Japan were slow and tedious. But I managed to get him intrigued enough to want to see Jurong Island for himself. When he came, our proposed site for him was still largely under water. He stood on the parts which were already reclaimed. The sand was still moist. He gave his approval. For Malaysia, there's no shortage of land. For Saudi Arabia, there's no shortage of land. Everybody's got land. But for us, we had to create the land. That's why Jurong Island is a unique example of creating something from nothing. There's that Disney song "Under the Sea", right?[33] It was my favourite song.

Q   *What motivated you to sell the project so relentlessly?*

A   I'm a salesman. When you ask me to sell, I will do it. If you ask me to bring someone to hell or heaven, I will do it. I won't waste time asking you why this person is going to hell or going to heaven. I cannot question myself. Lucio Noto likes to joke that he got conned by Philip Yeo several times. He said: "Every time he conned me, I ended up with a project in Singapore." But that's my job right? Anyway, the word "con" comes from "convince". So I'm not a conman. To these CEOs, I was their point man. I was the the one who hustled them. So they remember me. I have to make sure the customer is happy. You want repeat business. Unfortunately, the Admin Officer is not trained that way. Their job is to analyse and question: why do this, why do that? My favourite question is: why not?

---

33   The song was from animated film *The Little Mermaid*. It won the Academy Award for Best Original Song in 1989.

Q   *When Jurong Island opened officially in 2000, you mentioned in media reports that you had to "fend off protests" from various government ministries and departments during the construction. What happened?*

A   Everybody said it was a crazy idea. Who's going to come? JTC was not keen to start reclamation because they said there were no customers. But my argument was that if there was no land, how could there be customers? When people say I'm crazy, it means they did not want to do whatever I wanted to do. Cautious people don't want to do it. For me, when it's crazy, it means I'm required to push, to try. It's something which I can succeed in if I learn and push. But almost everyone wanted to see results before they would help. They asked me to show them the customers. So we had to sell ahead and it was a tough job.

Q   *Can you cite an example?*

A   I wanted to build a bridge, a causeway linking Jurong Island to the mainland. But other agencies were asking: "Oh, do you really need a bridge, why do you want to build a bridge, how many people cross that bridge, how many people use it." It was delayed for three years. Meanwhile, the island relied on ferry services which were clearly not as efficient. When then-Deputy Prime Minister Lee Hsien Loong opened the bridge in 2000, he said it was a mistake not to build the bridge earlier. The government was worried that the traffic on the bridge was too light to justify the investment.

Q   *How did you get manage to get Indonesian gas to Jurong Island?*

A   It was a first, a landmark deal. PUB didn't want to come in, didn't want to get involved. So what can I do? One of the investors needed natural gas as a feedstock. I found out natural gas fields were being developed in West Natuna, which is about 480km north-east of Singapore. So I wanted to buy gas from the Indonesians and pipe it to Jurong Island. Some people laughed at me. They said there was no way the Indonesians would agree. This was 1998 and Habibie had just become president. Mr Lee Kuan Yew said that rupiah would fall if Habibie became president and Habibie was very upset. That was when he called Singapore a "red dot". These people had no idea Habibie and I went all the way back. So I called him.

"Pak Habibie, can I visit you?" I asked.

"Okay, why do you want to come?" replied Habibie.

"I need to ask you for a job."

"Hahaha, okay okay, come and see me."

I reached Jakarta and explained to him about the West Natuna gas fields.

"You mean this is your project?" Habibie asked me.

"Yes it is," I replied.

"No problem."

He called a press conference and told everyone: "This is Pak Philip. He is my younger brother. Whatever he wants, whatever he does, I support him."[34] In January 1999, Singapore and Indonesia signed a 22-year agreement. Singapore would import 325 million standard cubic feet of natural gas every day. It was delivered through a 640-km pipeline. I created a company, Sembcorp Gas, to sign the agreement. During the signing, the Indonesians had my good friend, Minister of Mines and Energy Kuntoro Mangkusubroto. I

142

---

34 Yeo had publicly referred to Habibie as his "good friend and a big brother". See *The Business Times*, *"Indon firms will gain from Natuna pipeline: EDB chief"*, September 2, 1998.

represented Singapore. No Singaporean politician was there.

Remember my "two hands"? For Jurong Island, the two hands were EDB and Sembcorp. I had no choice. JTC couldn't do it. PUB was not interested. I was conveniently chairman of Sembcorp so I used it. Some people accused me of using Sembcorp for the sake of EDB. I had a job to do and my job was to create jobs. Legally or illegally, whether I have the authority or not, I would do it.

Q *You said before that Jurong Island was too difficult and in your next life you would rather be reborn in a bigger country?*

A Yes, I would rather be reborn in Ningbo, China.[35]

Q *China?*

A There is an island called Daxie, off Ningbo, about 3,500 hectares. No need to reclaim any land! When we were developing Jurong Island, they were also trying to turn it into a petrochemical island. They approached me for help but I wasn't keen. As far as I know, the island is still stuck and hasn't made much progress.

Q
&
A

143

---

35 Ningbo is a coastal city in China's Zhejiang province.

The legacy of Jurong Island has continued till today. It has drawn more than S$47 billion in investments. The energy and chemicals sector is the largest contributor to Singapore's manufacturing output, employing 26,000 people. The island has come to "epitomise the spirit of Singapore as well as our pioneer generation", said JTC's Ko. Yeo deserves a large chunk of credit. As Lee Hsien Loong said when opening the Jurong causeway, the key to the island's success was "entrepreneurship, conceiving the project, translating the vision into reality, and taking the risks involved in such an ambitious venture". And Yeo, said Ko in an interview with *The Straits Times* in 2000, was Singapore Inc's "singular entrepreneur".

144

Yeo's vision and clarity were critical to the success of not only Jurong Island, said those close to him, but also other seemingly outrageous adventures. "The single most important attribute that makes a project work is clarity. Philip Yeo has the ideas and he makes it simple. He would have something to describe his vision that's simple enough for people to understand. These ideas would drive a lot of other things including infrastructure and marketing," said former JTC chairman Lim Neo Chian. "With Jurong Island, his vision was a petrochemical hub that would produce 3,000,000 tonnes ethylene, three crackers and 70 companies interconnected with common services. And he just kept repeating that everywhere he went. He would say the same things whether it's to investors or his own people. He says it again and again and again. That helped to ensure that everybody worked on the same common idea. That helped to push the project a lot." The power of the vision, said former EDB officer Lisa Ooi, provided a galvanising force. "He cleared the path towards that vision, making sure all agencies understood," she said. "And everyone just *chiong*."[36] By the time Jurong Island opened officially in 2000, Yeo was ready not only to leave the project, but his long association with EDB. He would take his chemical romance a further step forward, going downstream into the realm of biomedical sciences. He called it his last hurrah.

145

---

36   *Chiong* is a Hokkien word which means "to charge ahead".

to live

7

The Ultimate Challenge

"I can't find a better man to do this job."

Trade and Industry Minister George Yeo on having Philip Yeo take charge of Singapore's push into life sciences, in a press statement at the Life Science Executive Committee Meeting in Singapore on June 24, 2000

It was the end of another overseas work trip when the coughing got louder and more persistent. The almost incessant wheezing caught Philip Yeo's attention. It came from Tsao Chieh, his special assistant for technology at Sembcorp. The 43-year-old had been a trusted aide for years since Mindef days. He was an SAF scholar who specialised in electronic countermeasures like radar systems and jamming. The composer was also "the acoustic expert" to Goh Keng Swee, recalled Yeo, who said Tsao was a favourite of the Old Guard minister. Tsao was "highly talented", said Yeo. He picked up four graduate degrees from Stanford University – a PhD in digital signal processing and three Masters in music, mathematics and electrical engineering – in a record-breaking five years. But on that fateful day in 1996, his life would take an unfortunate turn. "You'd better go see a doctor," said Yeo, who was the Sembcorp chairman.

The diagnosis was liver cancer. Yeo was floored, but refused to accept a death sentence for Tsao. Through his contacts, he found out there was an experimental drug on clinical trials in the United States. It required special approval for use in Singapore and Yeo managed to get the Ministry of Health permanent secretary Kwa Soon Bee to permit immediate import. It was the only possible cure and Tsao's family and friends were placing all their hopes in that tiny vial. Alas, it did not work. Tsao developed an allergy to it and reacted violently. "I slumped onto my chair upon hearing this news. There I was, watching a bright young life pass by before me and there was nothing I could do!" said Yeo in *Heartwork*. The treatment was stopped. By October, less than six months after the diagnosis, Tsao died. He was survived by his wife and two children. The degeneration was "very fast", said Yeo repeatedly. "I was shocked," he said. "I felt a personal loss with Tsao Chieh. By October, he was gone ..." His voice trailed, in perhaps the only emotional moment he allowed himself during the 10 interviews for this book.

But he was determined that the loss would not be in vain. Tsao's death rekindled a long-held interest in medicine. When Yeo was in the first year of pre-university studies, he had initially signed up for medical studies. But after three months, when he realised there were no overseas scholarships in medicine, he made the switch to science. "I wanted to fix people," he said. "I don't think I would make a good doctor because I don't have the patience. But I was interested in finding cures and treatments." He would find opportunities to pursue the hobby through his career in the public service, even skirting rules on some occasions and drawing public flak.

In 1986, when there was hardly any official funding for research and development (R&D) in life sciences in Singapore, Yeo gave S$40 million to set up the Institute of Molecular and Cell Biology (IMCB). It was his good old sleight of hand, taking the money from the Skills Development Fund (SDF), which he chaired, to set up the institute. "I put S$40 million but I gave one condition: In two years, we bring back the money, because it's money from

149

the SDF," he said in an interview with *The Straits Times* in 2000. The move drew criticism of impropriety from a reader of the newspaper in a published letter. The money was repaid when the institute obtained other funding.

But Yeo was not deterred. In 1988, as chairman of EDB, he set up a unit in the board to look at biotech promotion. A year later, in 1989, he proposed to the Ministry of Trade and Industry to take over the Science Council from the Ministry of Education and upgrade it. It was more than an administrative transfer. The aim was to transform science from an educational endeavour into one which serves the industry. In 1990, the Ministry of Trade and Industry formed the National Science and Technology Board (NSTB), the predecessor to A*STAR. Seven years later, Yeo helped fund the Cancer Therapeutics Research Group (CTRG) at the National University of Singapore (NUS) to establish that there is an Asian phenotype and also to prove that Asians react differently to diseases and drugs.

These brief flirtations with science and medicine sustained Yeo for years. But the death of Tsao led him to a rethink. Yeo wanted a more lasting relationship with this old romance. He wanted to go beyond drawing biomedical sciences investments to Singapore. He wanted more than just an ad-hoc advisory role. He saw biomedical sciences as the new frontier for himself and for Singapore, a sector which could not only create jobs but also save lives. And he wanted to commit himself to this passion completely. He wanted to find a cure, in particular for cancer. "I looked at Tsao Chieh and he went away so quickly," he said. "Why couldn't we do something about it? Why couldn't we focus on cancer research and find the human genome of cancer?"

He called it Singapore's "ultimate challenge" – the quest to save lives. "When you do engineering, you don't deal with life. When you deal with energy, you are working with coal, wood, oil. But medical science is ultimately about lives. When you go to a hospital, you're dealing with lives," he said. It is also "the most complex" from a technological point of view, he added. "If I want to challenge Singapore to be above our neighbours, I would choose an area where it's hard to build up. If I succeed, there is a high barrier to entry. Why choose something that people can duplicate? You choose the hardest one, and make sure you can make it."

The plan was to build up yet another cluster, just like he did with Jurong Island. And while the aim was to find cures, Yeo never forgot his other lifelong mission to create jobs. The biomedical sciences adventure he had in mind would have four prongs. The first is to help anchor the manufacturing of major pharmaceuticals in Singapore. While the likes of GlaxoSmithKline (GSK) has been in Singapore for decades, the aim was to entice these giants to enhance their operations, adding research to manufacturing. Top scientist Edward Holmes, who is the executive deputy chairman of the Biomedical Research Council in A*STAR, said: "If they could be encouraged to also develop a research component as well as the manufacturing component, it would help to keep the manufacturing in Singapore."

Second, R&D creates jobs and more importantly, high-value jobs. The value-add per worker in biomedical sciences is estimated at S$1.5m a year, doubling the S$700,000 in petrochemical. It also generates research-related employment, such as nursing, data analysis and a downstream flow of jobs. Third, through collaborations with the MNCs, it would encourage start-ups in Singapore. Yeo's vision was to develop intellectual property in Singapore through research and use that to create indigeneous companies. An example would be local medical diagnostic firm Restalyst, which successfully

151

commercialised a technology from the NUS and launched a more accurate new gastric cancer screening kit in late 2015.

Such solutions, said Professor John Wong, who is the CEO of the National University Health System, are the goal of Singapore' biomedical sciences push. "If you start developing solutions, companies come. Companies want to work with smart people," he said. "Companies want to work with people who can develop solutions. Everyone is looking for innovation." The energy and ideas of these start-ups would further help tie the MNCs to Singapore. Said Holmes: "The MNCs get a lot of their ideas from start-up companies. You can form a company and then these big guys come in and buy them up. When you have a lot of such start-ups, the big firms will not be far away."

Fourth, it would improve the health of Singaporeans in the long term. The aim is for the research to translate into clinical trials, which would then bring therapies to patients. This offers Singaporeans options which they might otherwise not have. "A great deal of the benefits of the bioscience effort would be in terms of the innovations that it brings to the Singapore healthcare system," said NUS president Tan Chorh Chuan. By locating the research in Singapore, it would help produce drugs which are not only Caucasian and Western-centric, but also cater to the genetic make-up of Asians. In liver cancer, for example, the mutation in the gene is different in Asians compared to Caucasians. A genetic test kit for the disease that is made in the West may not spot the disease in Asians. "In nearly every disease we've studied, we've found a difference between expression in a Caucasian population and expression in Asians," said Wong. "And it's not surprising. The colour of our hair is different. It's naive to think that what's going on inside should not be different. If our disease behaves differently and the drugs differently, it is very important for us to be in that position to study them."

Singapore's multiracial mix of Chinese, Malay and Indian offers a pool of data for Asian-focused research, which could translate into Asian-centric treatments and hopefully even decrease the cost of healthcare. The country also has the added advantage of being compact, has good record-keeping, respects the rule of law, international ethics and intellectual property and high-quality practice of medicine. "When you've got an ability to follow people from birth to death with one IC number and that IC number gives you all the medical records, X-rays and prescriptions, it is a great platform to do such research," said Wong, referring to how easy it is to track citizens via the unique number sequence on the IC, the acronym for "identity cards", which all Singaporeans carry.

The four targets formed the new biomedical sciences cluster, a "powerful" combination, said Holmes. As is typical of Yeo, an idea does not hibernate in his mind for long. After Jurong Island took off and he turned down Hong Kong tycoon Richard Li's multi-million dollar offer in 2000 – which was his fourth escape attempt from the civil service – he dived completely into biomedical sciences work. In February 2001, he became co-chairman of EDB and relinquished most of the work to Teo Ming Kian. Yeo would focus only on the biomedical sciences area of EDB. He also took on the chairmanship of NSTB and restructured it a year later as A*STAR. "NSTB was such a bad and unpronounceable name," he said. "I wanted a name which starts with a higher letter in the alphabet. I also wanted to draw the best and the brightest. When you sit for your PSLE, the best score is A star, right? That's the name I wanted," he added, referring to the Primary School Leaving Examinations taken by most Singaporean children at age 12.

153

He devoured medical journals and magazines, and bought and read books furiously. He even went through *Genetics for Dummies* and enjoyed the cartoon-based text. When those proved insufficient, he went back to school for five days. The NUS put together a crash course on molecular biology, dragging "14 other poor souls", in his words, with him. They included then-Minister of State for Trade and Industry Lim Swee Say. "Some people have superficial knowledge but Philip doesn't," said cancer researcher Sir David Lane. "He has detailed knowledge and can even discuss issues such as splicing. He's ahead of me."

If there was anything which Yeo did not understand, he was not embarrassed to call someone from NUS and IMCB for a crash explanation or course on cancer genetics and immunology in his office. He offered free lunch as tuition fee. "So while other people of my age were chasing after the white ball on the greens, I was reading up on immunotherapy," he said in *Heartwork*. It paid off quickly. Said Wong: "When we first started biomedical sciences, Philip's knowledge of molecular biology was like any informed lay person. Within five years, Philip knew molecular biology at a level which I would say was comparable to many people in science."

While the sector was relatively new to Yeo, he saw familiar spots. Biomedical sciences, in his view, was an amalgamation of two fields close to his heart: computing and engineering. "In a hospital room, there is a lot of equipment and that's engineering," he said. "And I see the human genome as a computer programme. The main programme is the DNA and the human chromosomes are sub programmes. So the best people to do biology today are actually computer scientists because you have to look at the chromosomes."

Computing was familiar ground. Yeo was the founding chairman of the

National Computer Board (NCB) in 1981 and had long been regarded in the civil service as a pioneer of computers. An often-told story was from his days in Mindef. At that time, only the Ministry of Finance was allowed to have its own mainframe computer. No other ministry was allowed to have its own IT department. Yeo got around this decree at Mindef, buying an IBM 4341 but calling it an "intermediate business machine" and removed all mention of "computers" in official documents. His cheeky play with the IBM acronym hookwinked the authorities. As Transport Minister Khaw Boon Wan recalled in a speech in 2003: "He got away with it! This covert operation became the foundation for Mindef's systems engineers who subsequently led the national computerisation effort of Singapore."

As NCB chairman, Yeo led an ambitious plan to carpet bomb the civil service with computers in one fell swoop. Instead of a piecemeal approach, he decided to wire up 10 ministries at one go. The private sector was salivating at the S$100 million budget. But when Yeo asked if they would be responsible for glitches and failures, they declined, saying they played only an advisory role. Yeo famously said: "Whose head is on the chopping block? If it's my head, I'd better do it myself." But it was an outrageously bold move since there were only about 850 IT professionals in the whole of Singapore. NCB recruited relentlessly, even taking in those from non IT backgrounds, and completed the computerisation in five years. "Well, Philip Yeo did not lose his head," said Khaw. "The Civil Service Computerisation Programme (CSCP) was a runaway success. Philip Yeo thinks big."

Yeo did not let up on his passion for computers. He was also a pioneer in the use of e-mail in the public sector. When it was introduced in EDB, senior officials refused to use them. "Personal computers were not used after being installed," said David Lim, an NCB old boy who moved to EDB and was tasked to look at the EDB's computerisation in 1986. "Nice big paperweights on desk." But Yeo started sending out e-mails and the others were forced to follow so as not to be left out of the loop. "Poof! All PCs were turned on," said Lim. Years later, in 1996, Yeo wrote Internet history when he launched Pacific Internet under Sembcorp and listed it on Nasdaq. The now defunct firm was at one point worth a billion dollars in 1999. But Yeo did not take a share of the company and profit from the listing.

The connection to computing and engineering gave him greater confidence to pursue the ultimate challenge of biomedical sciences. For it to succeed, he was determined that the sector must have a home in Singapore – the biomedical sciences version of chemicals at Jurong Island, if you will. He spotted a familiar old stomping ground – Portsdown Road, in a large former British army enclave in western Singapore. Some 35 years after he pushed unwanted public buses onto Portsdown as chairman of Singapore Automotive Engineering, he would return to the infamous scene. The authorities had zoned the Buona Vista area as a science hub in 2000 and Yeo quickly chose a large piece of vacant state land off Portsdown Road to build his biomedical sciences empire. He called it Biopolis: seven buildings, all interconnected, two million square feet of biolab space. "He likes playing with outrageous ideas as all innovative people do," said Sir David.

Yeo, who lacked the funds, did not seek government approval to build Biopolis. NSTB owned 60 per cent of the land, with JTC taking up the remainder. He transferred NSTB's shares to JTC as construction payment and convinced landlord JTC to a build and lease arrangement. JTC would build the complex and Yeo's A*STAR commited to a 10-year lease. "Look, JTC needed tenants and I created the tenants. JTC would never build anything unless there are tenants," he said. He was a most demanding tenant. He requested for monthly updates and wanted Biopolis ready in two years. Said JTC chairman Lim Neo Chian: "He was so impatient. If you want to build something in two years, you can't adopt the usual method of tender and design. We did a shortcut – build and lease."

Thankfully, in Lim Neo Chian, he had a partner who had known him since the Mindef days and often shared his philosophy of speed, action and vision. As Lim shared candidly: "I can see his logic. If you want to do something, do it quick. If you can do it in two years, why do you need three?" More importantly, Lim agreed with Yeo that Biopolis was more than just a physical space. It was a statement from Singapore to the rest of the world. "It's a way of telling the world that biomedical sciences research is very important, we are building seven buildings and it will be ready in two years," he said. "It was the same with Jurong Island, reclaiming seven islands to show how serious Singapore was. The message to the world was the same: Trust Singapore, don't worry, we will get it done for you." Tan Chorh Chuan, who was then dean of the NUS medical school, called Biopolis the "iconic symbol" of Singapore's biomedical sciences ambitions. "It became the most tangible signal to the rest of the world about the seriousness and the speed at which Singapore was pursuing this thrust," he said.

It was done at the usual Philip Yeo speed. The construction of Biopolis broke ground in December 2001. The steel and glass complex opened in October 2003. It was the Batam acceleration all over again. "In every other country I know of, you will take at least two to three years of planning," said Nobel laureate biologist Sydney Brenner, who was a key adviser to Yeo. "So people were amazed. There was nothing where Biopolis is. We were deep in mud. I was very impressed by how fast everything went." When A*STAR moved into its new base in 2003, its various institutes took up home in buildings named Nanos, Genome, Helios, Chromos, Proteos, Matrix and Centros – a homage to the long history of science from its roots in ancient Greece. All seven buildings share the same basement and are linked by bridges, an "angular jigsaw puzzle" said *Bio-IT World* magazine. The idea was copied from Sweden. On a trip to the Nordic country, Yeo noticed interconnected buildings for the scientists and found out it was to shelter the residents from the bitter winter. Yeo wanted to protect Biopolis researchers from the sun and rain of the tropics.

The integrated hub was more than just hardware. Yeo was intent on cross-fertilisation. He wanted research to blend into industry. "He could understand the critical importance of agglomeration effects – that when you bring together talent into a physical site, allow them to interact, and if we bring in not just academics but also industry and link them up with hospitals, you get a lot of very positive spillover effects," said Tan.

Biopolis now houses A*STAR research institutes and also major research arms of pharmaceutical companies. In 2008, for instance, American pharmaceutical giant Eli Lilly opened its research labs across two buildings in Biopolis. The likes of GSK, PerkinElmer, Nestle, Danone and Abbott also started research work in Singapore. It has led to scientists moving into companies. At the Bioprocessing Technology Institute (BTI) of A*STAR, for instance, close to 140 staff made the crossover in the last decade. "For us, it is good that we have a turnover of scientists to refresh the institute and, frequently, when these scientists go into industry, they become our ambassadors," said BTI executive director Lam Kong Peng in *The Sunday Times* in 2015.

The results have been sterling. Singapore's biomedical sciences industry output has grown from S$6.3 billion in 2000 to S$21.5 billion in 2014. It contributes some 4 to 5 per cent of GDP and employs 23,000 people. In the financial year 2011 to 2013, A*STAR generated 292 patents per billion of spending on R&D, more than the likes of Harvard and the Massachusetts Institute of Technology. By 2015, Biopolis and Fusionopolis campuses were hosting 16,000 scientists, researchers and innovators from the private and public sectors. Experts believe much more is to come. "The amount of money biomedical sciences brings to Singapore is a significant part of the GDP," said former GSK chairman Richard Sykes. "But you can't just measure it in a linear fashion. Biomedical sciences is completely different from chip technology where you can make chips tomorrow. You can't make drugs tomorrow or change medicine tomorrow. It's a long-term investment." Tan credits Yeo for the success. "He'll always be remembered as the person who built it," he said. "The subsequent development of the whole sector owes a great deal to his vision, energy and abilities in those very important years."

But the push into biomedical sciences was not without critics. In 2007, a powerful critic in Singapore slammed the multi-billion investment as a waste of taxpayers' money. Lee Wei Ling, daughter of Lee Kuan Yew and younger sister of Prime Minister Lee Hsien Loong, criticised that resources were spread too thinly. The head of the National Neuroscience Institute added that Singapore should focus on niche areas such as hepatitis B and head injuries, instead of competing with the West on big-name research. The outspoken doctor said, in an interview with Reuters, that she had shared her concerns with her father and that Singapore's biomedical sciences push had not achieved significant breakthroughs despite the investments. The impressive numbers did not impress her either. It was illogical to credit the industry performance to the research drive, she told the media. Drug companies were drawn to Singapore because of generous government help, strict enforcement of intellectual property laws and an educated workforce. It had little to do with money pumped into research.

Yeo, predictably, did not hold back too. He pointed out that Lee had never stepped into the Biopolis and did not understand that biomedical sciences requires long-term investment without quick returns. She was "one voice in the wilderness", he said, adding that he had better things to do than address the concerns of a complainant. "How many people get head injuries? Get hepatitis? Young kids after 1987 have been vaccinated. Hepatitis is not relevant to us. Head injuries? Unless you bang your head against the wall ..." he said.

She insisted she was not a lone voice and that she had received dozens of e-mail and messages from local doctors and researchers supporting her. She fired back: "I would say that Mr Philip Yeo, having never practised as a doctor, is strategising about biomedical sciences research directions in an ivory tower. That is why he can dismiss hepatitis B and head injury as unimportant. Head injury is one of the leading causes of death and disability in young people. He has been very successful in selling Singapore in the past, but biomedical sciences research is a different ball game." She added: "This is not a matter of one-upmanship. We're talking about billions of dollars of tax-payers' money. I will not let this mistake continue."

Reactions were mixed. Some pointed out that indeed, none of the

160

pharmaceuticals or devices were ready for the production line. The World Bank also said in late 2006 that Singapore had a 50-50 chance of succeeding in its drive, citing a lack of scale and long gestation periods among the challenges. But others, like Sir Richard, argued that research is a long-term process and Singapore was on the right path. They said that Singapore had already targeted niche areas important and relevant to Asians, such as liver and gastric cancers. Said scientist Edward Holmes: "The focus has been on what we can do in Singapore that we can't do in the US and in the UK. While Singapore is a tiny place, it represents probably a quarter of the world's population if you think of the Chinese, the Malay and Indian populations here. We have picked disorders like gastric cancer, diabetes, glaucoma. I think Singapore has been smart, picking something that we can do that can be impactful for a very large proportion of the world's population."

161

The government came out on the side of Yeo. The Ministry of Trade and Industry issued a statement saying that "our biomedical effort is heading in the right direction, but we will continue to fine-tune our policies as we gain more experience". Prime Minister Lee Hsien Loong gave the biomedical sciences push his backing too. A month after the spat first surfaced publicly, he said in March 2007: "It's early days yet but I think we've made significant progress. We've made significant progress because we've been able to bring to Singapore very high quality scientific talent – people who are at the peak of their careers, who are productive, who have uprooted themselves to come to Singapore and work in Singapore."

Prime Minister Lee stressed that the "biomed drive isn't *masak-masak*", a Singlish term for "child's play", and emphasised the importance of the cluster which biomedical sciences engenders. "You are not just talking about every discovery leading to a drug or a new treatment. But you are talking about a whole climate of discovery or innovations, which will enable us to have not just research institutes, but pharmaceutical companies, other biomedical sciences companies, very high quality medical clusters in universities, very high quality medical services sector in Singapore – leading to foreigners coming here for treatment, leading to foreign scientists coming here for research work, leading to Singaporeans going into the sector."

The results are, slowly, proving the authorities and Yeo right. In 2012, for instance, A*STAR scientists made a breakthrough in Chikungunya research. The mosquito-borne, infectious disease is endemic to South-east Asia and Africa. It is an example of the targeted research neglected by the rest of the world but important to Singaporeans and those in the region. Two years later, the first made-in-Singapore genetic test for corneal stromal dystrophy, where proteins clump together in the cornea and affect vision, was made. It was part of the Polaris programme, a national scheme to translate biomedical sciences research findings into treatments for patients in Singapore. In the same year, researchers at A*STAR's Institute of Medical Biology found new clues to early detection and precision treatment of ovarian cancer. The lack of symptoms unique to ovarian cancer makes it one of the most difficult cancers for early diagnosis.

Cancer specialist John Wong believes such progress is especially crucial as Singapore becomes an ageing nation. "Our goal is to try and change the natural history of the disease. Yes, we all have to get old, but there's nothing which says we've to get old with high blood pressure, diabetes, cancer and heart attacks," he said. "If we want Japan to do all the R&D and we import the results from Japan, it might work, but that means we'll always be 15 years

162

behind Japan. Or we can be actually working to solve the problem ourselves. To me, research is not a luxury. Research is a critical mindset whereby you start saying how can I do this better, how can I fix the problem, how do we become a nation with solutions rather than people who just basically say that's the way it is. Singapore is definitely on the right track with our biomedical push."

These small steps graduated into a great leap in 2015. In February, Singapore's homegrown MerLion Pharmaceuticals became the first in the country to have its new novel drug on ear infections approved by the United States Food and Drug Administration (FDA). MerLion is a joint venture between GSK and A*STAR's IMCB. In July, an even bigger breakthrough emerged, when a made-in-Singapore cancer drug entered clinical trial for the first time, offering hope to hundreds of patients each year suffering from a range of cancers, including colorectal, ovarian and pancreatic. These cancers share a common group of cell-signalling pathways known as Wnt signalling, which are known to promote cancer growth. The ETC-159, which is the name of the drug, works to inhibit these pathways, suppressing cancer proliferation and preventing cancer progression. "This drug candidate therefore offers a promising novel and targeted cancer therapy that could shape future cancer therapeutic strategies," said A*STAR and Duke-National University of Singapore Graduate Medical School (Duke-NUS) in a statement. The first patient received a dose of the drug on June 18, with 58 lined up in Phase 1 of the trials. Said Prof David Virshup, inaugural director of the Programme in Cancer and Stem Cell Biology at Duke-NUS: "It is fitting that Singaporeans might be the first to benefit from this Singapore-developed drug."

Q *Why did you decide that biomed was an area that Singapore should focus on?*

A There is a missing link in medical science. At one end, you have the scientists doing the research. They are only interested in knowledge and finding solutions. But they are not responsible for its implementation. They don't see patients. But science alone doesn't help people. You have to involve the doctors in the hospitals, which is on the other end of the spectrum. Yet hospitals are busy taking care of patients. The hospitals are like production lines – surgery, treatment. It has no time to experiment. Doctors are repair mechanics. They fix one patient at a time with drugs or with medical surgery and devices. Scientists are looking at solutions for everybody. So there's a big gap between basic science and hospitals. My aim was to fill this gap. The ultimate challenge is what is called "bench to bedside" – translational research. Now, the time taken from bench to bedside is between 20 to 30 years. It's very long.

If I'm a doctor working on, let's say, pancreatic cancer, I want to be able to work with a scientist who works on inflammation of the organs. So the doctor and the scientist have to come together. They need to combine their work. My purpose in biomedical sciences is to fill in this missing link by doing clinical trials. The scientist will provide the solution. The hospitals will provide the patients. Pharmaceuticals come in at this point. They are good at clinical trials. Let's say I found a new gene for, maybe, liver cancer. I need to try it on patients and I need to produce that drug. Who is going to pay for the drug? Pharmas will do that because clinical trials are very expensive. Universities and research institutes can't afford it. Only the big companies can do it.

Q   *How do A*STAR and Biopolis fit into this missing link?*

A   A*STAR's institutes groom researchers and do the science work. By housing them together with private research labs by the pharmas in Biopolis, they can collaborate for clinical trials. They are linked to the hospitals but they are not part of it. This allows them to do trials, including on animals. It is a triangular relationship: research institutes under A*STAR, major pharmas and hospitals under Ministry of Health. The hospital is the end point.

Q   *You were dealing with weapons and then industries. How different is biomed?*

A   In engineering, I was dealing with products. Biomed is about people and lives. Engineering doesn't do that – you make a product, and sell a product, there is no human clinical trials involved. Buy a phone, the phone doesn't work, you curse and swear at Apple, that's all. But if you put the wrong stent into your heart or blood vessel or even the brain for aneurysm, you kill people. Hey, this is not Nazism or Communism. You don't do experiments on people for fun.

Q   *Any particular area in biomed which you are most interested in?*

A   I read everything. There are all these articles I read about gut bacteria.

Q   *This morning I read an article about freezing your shit.*

A   When you have some gut problem in future, you should swallow the frozen shit. It kills all your bacteria. There is a lot written on microbiology. When you have a mobile phone or shoes, you have bacteria there. So through forensic science, you can identify a person through his bacteria. It's even better than finger prints. But I'm looking at it for the medical drug potential. There is great drug potential in your poop.

Q *In shit?*

A There's gold in shit. It's called the promise of poop. Hey, I'm serious. This is not a joke. Don't laugh. Fecal transplants offer hope of treating many diseases.

Q *Fecal transplant?*

A Yes, yes, yes. There are one or two guys in Singapore whom I could actually discuss these things with. Inflammation of the gut can lead to cancer – stomach cancer. Colon cancer is linked to the gut too. The gut also affects obesity. I've been reading these things for more than 10 years. Do you find civil servants today reading such things? I don't think so. They won't care about shit.

Q *Speaking of pungent stuff, you mentioned before that scientific research is like growing durian trees, which takes more than seven years to go from planting seeds to producing fruit. How long must Singapore wait to see a key breakthrough?*

A I would say about 25 years.

Q *That's a very long wait and you are not known to be patient.*

A We started in 2001 and I wanted to cultivate Singapore's own pool

166

of top scientists. It takes time. The first batch came back only in 2012. Three to four years for a bachelor degree, a year in our labs and then five to seven years to get a PhD. When we have our own scientists, I can go to the pharmaceutical companies and tell them: "Look, my talent is here." Singapore offers attractive tax incentives and fantastic infrastructure. Now, we also provide human capital.

Q *Why is human capital important?*

A It is an additional way to anchor the pharmas in Singapore. So if we discover a new drug in A*STAR, we will also own the intellectual properties and earn the royalties. If we remain a pure production base, there is little we can do to prevent the pharmas from uprooting and moving to another country. They come to Singapore because of our tax incentives. They don't have to be here. So by going into research, and having our own scientists, Singapore can build a cluster that goes beyond just manufacturing of drugs. Don't forget, even when our scientists make a breakthrough, they need the pharma companies to produce that drug. They also need the pharmas for clinical trials and for testing on sick people. Clinical trials are very expensive. Universities cannot do it.

If we were to find new treatments in cancer drugs, for example, we will be able to work with the pharmas on a higher level. We have more reasons to encourage them to build another plant here and start another development production here. Pharma companies are by nature conservative. If this drug works, they will produce and sell the same thing for years. It is very risky for them to switch to a new drug because every drug takes a lot of time and money.

Q *But what's to stop them from taking Singapore's discovery and moving their production to China?*

A   We own the intellectual property (IP). We are unable to take it to the market because we are not a pharma company. But because we own the IP, we can set conditions and make sure that production remains in Singapore.

Q   *What was the idea behind Biopolis?*

A   I chose the name and I wanted to use the word "polis". It is a Greek word which means a city of 20,000 people. Any population more than 20,000 and they had to leave to create another one because 20,000 is a sustainable population. It's like a big village. So there were polis all over the whole of the Mediterranean, including one called Lesbos. You know, Lesbos Island, where all the Syrian refugees rushed to? You know what Lesbos stands for? That's where the word lesbian comes from.

Q   *Really? I didn't know that.*

A   Lesbos was one of the early city states where they set up the first all-girl school. In those days, girls didn't go to school. So Lesbos became a derivative for lesbian. I like to read Greek stuff although I've never been to Greece. A lot of things about Western civilisation were borrowed from the Greeks.

Q   *Okay, back to Biopolis. What was the idea behind the complex?*

A   There are seven buildings and if you pay attention, you would notice that the buildings do not carry the names of the research institutes. They are called Matrix, Proteos ... scientific names. So, for example, I didn't allow IMCB to put their name and called it the "IMCB

Building". That would have been the normal way in Singapore. It was a deliberate decision because I wanted each building to have both public research institutes and private research institutes. I wanted a crossover between both sides so that both sides collaborate, talk to each other and share ideas.

Singapore is the only research place where companies and private research are co-located with public research institutes. There is no such model in the world. In other countries, they are bigger and they have no need to co-locate public and private institutions. But to me, it makes no sense. See, if you go to NUS and NTU,[37] there are no companies there. If I were running NUS now, I would allow companies to have their research labs there and I would subsidise them, provided they employ my students and create future work.

Q *What's the difference between Biopolis and Fusionopolis?*

A Biopolis is all biomedical sciences. Fusionopolis is engineering – fusion of engineering. Fusionopolis is the physical science sequel. It has semiconductor and material science. It has its own MRT[38] station – one-north.

Q *It is the only MRT station with a name that starts with a lower-case letter.*

A Well, it is quite a strange station. In the original masterplan of the Circle Line, there was no station here. To be fair, it is a very short distance between Buona Vista and Kent Ridge stations. I told MRT to build a station here but they refused. They said they don't have the budget for it. So I asked JTC to pay for the construction of the station. We chose a spot directly above the station. Without the

---

37 Nanyang Technological University
38 MRT is an acronym for Mass Rapid Transit – Singapore's subway system.

station, we have no connection. I didn't bother waiting for approval. I just got it done. Who would dare to do such things these days? You see, my EDB office was at Raffles City, which is directly above the City Hall MRT station. It was so convenient. Many people took the MRT to work.

Despite the plans of an almost airtight biomedical sciences cluster and the ambitious Biopolis and Fusionopolis, the ultimate challenge to build up the sector needed the most critical ingredient: talent. As Yeo said: "You know, what is research? It's talent. Buildings are great. But you need the people." The hardware of Biopolis, for instance, acted as a magnet to attract talent. "If I wanted to attract young people to research, I needed to give them something to aspire to. That's why I built Biopolis. It's their home," he said.

He had an ambitious target: to groom 1,000 Singaporean researchers in a decade. Or as Senior Minister of State Josephine Teo, who was a former human resource director of A*STAR, described it, "a battalion of scientists". Yeo would provide them them with scholarships to pursue PhDs. "I've given more scholarships than anybody else in Singapore," he said. It is most likely true, although it is an assertion that is difficult to verify. What is certain though, is that Yeo is most closely associated with scholarships in the minds of many Singaporeans. And the reason is because of an unprecedented public spat between a politician and a civil servant in a country where fissures among the elite are rarely exposed.

8

The Talent Thief

"He likes to collect people."

Minister for Manpower Lim Swee Say on Philip Yeo, in a 2015 interview for this book

E ight months after the biggest financial crisis to hit Asia in more than two decades, the Singapore legislature sat to map out its plan for the year. It was March 1998 and the region was being roiled by the devastated economies of Thailand, South Korea and Indonesia. Singapore, sandwiched between a fallen Jakarta and an ailing Kuala Lumpur, was shaken. Its government, famously quick in reacting to global changes, swiftly set out its agenda to protect the economy, save jobs and bolster investors' and Singaporeans' confidence. But the announcements didn't garner the attention they deserved. Instead, the much-anticipated Budget was hijacked by a spectacular spat between a veteran politician and a senior civil servant.

It started innocuously enough. Chng Hee Kok, a four-term Member of Parliament (MP), gave a speech about the importance of talent management and retention, citing American multinational firms as role models. Midway, he pivoted to the local scene, criticising two statutory boards for naming and shaming three scholarship holders who had terminated their bonds recently. "Have we been too harsh? Contrast this approach with that of the 100 best corporations in America," he said.

Scholarship has been the preferred vehicle for the Singapore government to uncover and groom both young elite politicians and civil servants, with most of its Cabinet and top bureaucrats made up of scholarship holders, or "scholars" in local parlance. The scholarships invariably come with a bond to work in the civil service and early termination carries a financial penalty. Two government bodies, the EDB and the National Computer Board (NCB), had decided to take the unprecedented step of naming the bond breakers in Singapore's major newspapers.

Chng's criticism was not surprising. The naming move had been controversial and Singaporeans had debated its merits animatedly. Chng himself had made a similar argument in a public speech five months earlier, in October 1997. But what he revealed subsequently in his Parliament speech stunned many. He said that after his first speech, he was invited to a breakfast meeting with senior officials of the two statutory boards. "Amongst many things said to me at this breakfast meeting, the most senior gentleman in the group accused me of sharing the values of these scholars and he said that if I shared the values of these scholars I should resign from public office. In other words, a civil servant telling an MP to resign," he said.

172

The revelation immediately seized the attention of those in the House and beyond. After probing by fellow long-time MP Tan Cheng Bock, Chng said he was told his name could be included in the name-and-shame statement and that he should have sent that first speech of his, made in October 1997, for vetting by the relevant authorities before delivery. "I want to assure Members of this House that in all my years as a Member of Parliament, no Minister or office-holder has ever asked me for my speech before I speak on any subject," he said. The "most senior gentleman" was the chairman of EDB. Chng did not mention his name. He didn't need to.

Everyone knew it was Philip Yeo.

An uproar erupted in Parliament. The Leader of the House, Wong Kan Seng, asked MPs to focus on the Budget and debate the bond-breaking issue in another session. "We should not use these two precious days for debating bond breakers because there are 45 MPs wanting to speak," he said. But the Speaker of Parliament, Tan Soo Khoon, allowed it. MPs lined up in support of Chng, lambasting not only the name-and-shame policy but also Yeo. Tan Cheng Bock, who later came close to winning the elected presidency in 2011, led the firing. He said that despite some MPs often expressing contrarian views to the government, they were never asked by the Prime Minister to resign. "Is he getting too big for his shoes?" he asked, a pointed reference to Yeo. The media splashed the debate on its front page. Afternoon tabloid *The New Paper*, which is more well-known for its coverage of sex scandals and soccer, put Yeo on its cover with the headline "Mr Let-fly".

Two EDB alumni-turned-politicians David Lim and Lim Swee Say defended their former boss. Lim Swee Say, who was chairman of NCB, pointed out a minor, but critical, detail in the debate which was largely ignored and has been largely forgotten since. The scholars named were not those who broke bonds in the midst of service, he said. They did not serve even a day of their bond before termination. David Lim argued that a scholarship is more than a commercial agreement to be settled by payment of money. It carries with it prestige and honour and "an equal measure of responsibility" to return to serve. He added that Chng did not tell the full story. "We have heard strong accusations about his improper conduct, within the protection of this House. But we did not hear why he said, what he said. Those who presented the story half-told would do justly to tell the

173

other half," said David Lim.

The other half was told by then-Deputy Prime Minister Lee Hsien Loong, in a statement on the issue in Parliament. He agreed with Lim Swee Say and David Lim, saying that scholarships are more than commercial deals and must carry moral responsibilities. Bond breaking had become a problem and the naming policy had his endorsement. "Unfortunately, there were no extenuating circumstances (for the three scholars who broke bonds)," he said. "All three were still studying, and had not even started work. They had no difficulties with their courses, or medical problems, or family difficulties. They made no effort to try to serve EDB or NCB. So finally, EDB and NCB decided that these three scholars had to be named. I vetted and approved the press statement."

On the breakfast meeting between Chng and Yeo, Lee distributed to the House notes taken by EDB. In it, it was revealed that Yeo had told Chng he urged his son to take up a scholarship only if he was serious about serving the bond. Otherwise, it would be unfair to other applicants and the sponsor of the scholarship. Yeo then asked Chng, whose daughter was studying in Yale University, if he would advise her differently. Chng replied if his daughter wanted to break bond, he would not be against it. At that point, Yeo told him he should resign as an MP as such views would send a wrong signal to Singaporeans.

Said Lee: "In other words, the issue was not whether or not we should publish the names of the bond breakers, which is a matter on which we may reasonably disagree. The issue was a fundamental one: whether or not there is anything wrong with breaking a scholarship bond, especially without making the slightest effort to fulfil it. It is clear from the file note that

Mr Chng had argued that it was quite all right to break a scholarship bond, because it was just a matter of a legal contract and liquidated damages, and this is what provoked the dispute with Mr Yeo." Lee added he had told Yeo it was wrong of him to ask an MP to resign. "I have reminded him that it is for the party leadership and the Whip, not Chairman of EDB, to take an MP to task," he said. But Chng's stance on bond breaking was wrong too, he added, and even "dangerous" if it became widely held.

Chng disputed the sequence of the breakfast meeting, saying Yeo had asked him to resign at the start of the meeing. "The starting point was he asked me to resign. And later on, in the middle, when I confirmed that a number of my colleagues shared similar views about naming scholars, because I had a lunch discussion in Parliament and a number of people do express that there is no need to name scholars, EDB Chairman said that they should do likewise. This was not in the file note," he said after Lee's speech. But he admitted he had reconsidered his position and that he would not encourage his children to break bonds.

The spat ended with both Yeo and Chng exchanging letters of apology which were made public. Yeo apologised for his remarks during the breakfast meeting and said he was glad Chng had changed his view. Chng apologised for his contribution to "this unfortunate episode". Yeo's letter was his only public comments on the incident, until this book (see the Q & A section of this chapter). As Lee said in Parliament: "I urge Members to exercise restraint in criticising civil servants, especially in this House. The civil servants are not here to defend themselves, nor can they answer back." The incident affected Yeo badly, said friends close to him. "It was the only instance when I saw him close to tears," said long-time EDB staff Khoo Seok Lin. "He was so upset that an MP would sanction bond breaking. It violated his values of loyalty and service to the country. But he knew he shouldn't have asked him to resign. He knew he had made a mistake and so he apologised."

He has the firm support of the EDB mafia. "Even today, when it comes to the bond-breaking issue, you will have many of us in EDB and outside who are firmly behind Philip Yeo on this and we'll be prepared to debate with anyone about that," said current EDB chairman Beh Swan Gin. "If you say you're prepared to commit to something, are you going to see it through? And the fight was all about that. For him, it was all about that." While Yeo stayed silent during the spat, his association with scholarships rang louder than ever. The high-profile squabble turned Mr EDB into Mr Scholarship in the eyes of many Singaporeans. He became a patron of sorts for scholarships, taking great pains to ensure the programme would continue and thrive. As former EDB managing director Ko Kheng Hwa said: "Everywhere Philip Yeo went, he either created or expanded on scholarships." Yeo is, said Lim Swee Say, "very consistent" when it comes to scholarships. But what has been less discussed as a corollary of the scholarships has been his near obsession with talent. In truth, scholarship was merely the conduit he preferred to get to the prize he wanted: talent.

The people who are close to him would liken it to a hobby. "When he knows of somebody whom he thinks can add value to whatever he's doing, he would collect them," said Lim Swee Say. "I was one of those. He got to know me when I was a young lieutenant in the Singapore Armed Forces and he decided to take me in as part of his collection." Long-time aide Seah Kia Ger would make the same observation. The Chinese-educated Nanyang University graduate got to know Yeo in Mindef and Yeo quickly identified him as a useful talent given his own lack of proficiency in Mandarin. Seah, who worked with Yeo at EDB and A*STAR, would become his key adviser and translator in matters related to China. He said: "Philip Yeo realised my command of the Chinese language would come in handy and he added me to his collection of people."

The talent collector gave himself a cheekier label. "One of my skills is kidnapping talent. If I were a criminal, I would be a very good one," said Yeo, only half-jokingly. The skills were honed consistently through his career, starting with his abductions of physically-unfit soldiers in the 1970s to make up the "systems engineers". But the sleight of hand which led to "Philip Yeo's illegals" in Mindef was only one of several tricks he had slowly perfected over the decades in his relentless hunt for talent.

He is also a master of persuasion. "He has a way of persuading people   177
to do certain things that obviously fits his plan," said former EDB deputy chairman Lim Neo Chian. Contrary to his usual haste, Yeo's strategy on talent hunting was surprisingly patient. "One inch at a time" was how Lim described it. "He doesn't like 'no' for an answer." Cancer expert Sir David Lane agreed, recounting how Yeo drew him to Singapore initially on a year-long sabbatical, before locking him down to a longer term job with A*STAR. "He is a very persistent man ... and, you know, he's just very good at persuading," he shared.

Usually, said Lim, it started with an e-mail. Without the unsuspecting person realising it, Yeo started including a target in e-mails on the subject or project which he believed the person could play a role in. "Actually you haven't agreed to anything. But he would keep sending you things and giving you files to read," said Lim. "And you would begin to spend time on it." Next,

Yeo would include the kidnap target in meetings. "Somehow, it was very hard to say no to a meeting," said Lim. "So you would attend the meeting. Then step by step, before you know it, he would lead you to a position where he wanted you to be. You would get sucked into a situation – it would almost be like you were 'conned' into it."

When persuasion could not be used, Yeo turned to sex appeal. Despite once being named among Singapore's sexiest men alive, he had the modesty, or good sense, to not rely on his own sensual attraction. But he was decidedly uncivil in his penchant for advertisements and models. To draw young Singaporeans to take up scholarships with A*STAR, he commissioned an advertising campaign with posters of a young man on a motorcycle in a leather vest with the words "Born to R&D" and a young woman with a human genome tattoo on her arm with the teasing question: "Got a burning passion for science?" The Eurasian model was a cover girl of men's magazine *FHM*. "I was selling passion through sex appeal. Can you imagine the PSC having an advertisement like this? No way!" he said as he roared with laughter, referring to the Public Service Commission. When the poster was put up in a top university in the United States, it was stolen. Said Barbara Morgan, wife of prominent chemical engineering scholar Charles Zukoski: "What amazed me was the poster of the young woman. Our son, who must have been 14 at the time, had that taped to his bedroom door!"

The full suite of talent-thieving skills was used by Yeo to build up the biomedical sciences industry in Singapore – sleight of hand, persuasion and sex appeal. His premise was that biomedical sciences is about people, or what he referred to as "two-legged assets", usually illustrated with a gesture of two fingers brisk walking across the table. Buildings and capital can do only so much without talent in research. He wanted to build up a core of Singaporean researchers, equip them with PhDs and have them groomed by a stellar cast of internationally-acclaimed scientists. Said NUS president Tan Chorh Chuan: "Biomedical sciences is about talent. It's a talent-dependent sector."

Yeo travelled the world to "kidnap" star scientists, whom he referred to as "whales". These top scientists are drawn to Singapore on fully-funded research grants and, in the case of renowned cancer researcher Edison Liu, even a dedicated building for his cancer genomics work – the Genome building in Biopolis. "The intention in whale attaction was to help raise the profile of Singapore's R&D capabilities," said Yeo in *Heartwork 2*, a book on EDB's success stories. "Singapore had no leader in the sector, and recruiting these senior figures would help to cultivate a robust R&D scene over time and provide invaluable connections to overseas networks." It worked. The shock of Liu's transfer sent out a clear statement of intent from Singapore. Said Professor John Wong, the CEO of the National University Health System, who helped recruit Liu: "When the news broke that Ed Liu was moving to Singapore, and this was just at the beginning of our biomedical initiative, I think that was one of the biggest catalysts for the whole biomedical initiative. The whole world, certainly the whole scientific world, took notice. If Ed Liu was going to move to Singapore, there must be something there."

His whale hunt was remarkably successful. He got Nobel laureate and biologist Sydney Brenner, a close friend and adviser behind the biomedical sciences push in Singapore, to put together the list. He prowled the world for the prized catches. Besides Liu, Yeo also managed to snag Sir David, cancer geneticists Neal Copeland and Nancy Jenkins, and cellular cardiologist Judy

179

Swain and her biomed scientist husband Edward Holmes, among others. While Liu, Copeland and Jenkins have since left, with grumblings of red tape and interference from bureaucrats, most of the whales successfully hunted by Yeo have remained and continued to contribute.

Holmes described Yeo's whirlwind abductions vividly. In 2006, on a trip to Singapore, Holmes was asked by Wong if he would consider moving to the country. Holmes laughingly replied: "Yeah, that would be fun." In two hours, Yeo called him and asked to have lunch. During lunch, Yeo asked Holmes and his wife to make the move. "Sure, sounds fantastic. Make me an offer," said Holmes. Two days later, after returning to San Diego in the United States, he received an e-mail from Yeo requesting for a meeting in Paris. "I said 'sure, I can go to Paris, sounds like fun'," said Holmes. They met in a dingy Vietnamese restaurant in the French capital and Yeo persuaded them to join A*STAR over wonton noodles and duck meat. "And so in typical Philip Yeo fashion, when I got back to San Diego there was a job offer by e-mail," he said. "It was classic. I can't think of anything more exciting than the year of 2006."

These whales served a larger purpose – to nurture young Singaporean scientists, whom he called "guppies". Yeo's plan was to jumpstart research through the whales, but bank on the guppies to build Singapore's biomedical sciences dreams. "When the young scientists come back, they will need somebody to be their supervisors," he said. "That's why I need the whales." Wong estimated that Singapore needed one generation's worth of mentors until the Singapore pipeline is developed. The Singapore core, added Holmes, was the true grand vision of Yeo in biomedical sciences. "It was to build up a Singapore pipeline in the long run. It's not about people from abroad."

Yeo's demands on the guppies were no less stringent than the whales. Only the best would do. "It was vital that selected candidates possess a kind of Spartan mental capacity and resolute determination," he said in *Heartwork 2*. "All candidates have to go through a rigorous selection process. They need to have not only impececcable academic records, but also a strong fighting spirit. It is imperative that these scholars are go-getting 'Type A' personalities." He once made a pair of identical twins duke it out for a PhD scholarship. "I told them there was only one scholarship and they had to fight among themselves to decide who would get it. It was to test their fighting spirit," he said with a loud chuckle. His fellow selectors called him cruel, only half jokingly. In the end, he gave it to both of them.

Such "supreme confidence is a must", he continued in *Heartwork 2*. "As the country's future economic prospects rest on their shoulders and they must have the drive and ambition to do bold, innovative science, and build business to take their science from lab to market. To put it frankly, I wanted a new generation of research and thought leaders, not test-tube cleaners." It is not surprising. After all, this is a man who had said he wanted scholars with not only brains but also the brawn of Arnold Schwarzenegger. "We should not have first-class scholars looking like water lilies ... then Singapore will become a library, not a nation," he said in a media interview in 1997.

To get this new generation of leaders, he chose a vehicle he was most familiar with and confident in: scholarships. He used it to good effect in his Mindef and NCB days and built on it significantly in EDB, actively seeking companies which would sponsor scholarships for Singaporeans. When Glaxo wanted to offer a gift to Singapore, he chose scholarships. Said Lim Swee Say: "Other people would say, 'why don't you give me a billion-dollar investment?' It would go into that person's report card. But that's not Philip Yeo. It's in his blood to nurture people." Despite the controversy of the spat with Chng in 1998, he was determined to pursue the same track in 2001.

But the biomedical sciences scholarships presented a far greater challenge than EDB's. While he gave out more than 30 scholarships a year at EDB, he wanted more than triple that number at A*STAR. His aim was 100 PhD scholarships a year over a decade, creating 1,000 PhD researchers in biomedical sciences, and science and technology in Singapore. He had no money for such an ambitious programme. Of course, that was hardly a deterrent. He did a sleight of hand again. In 2001, when he took over the National Science and Technology Board (NSTB), A*STAR's predecessor, he slashed 10 per cent of its research fund and used it for the scholarships. It amounted to S$1 billion. "I realised that there were no Singaporeans doing research in NSTB. I had to change that," he said.

182

When he gave out the first batch of scholarships, the authorities jumped. The PSC complained that A*STAR was stealing talent and there were orders from the Cabinet to seize his funds, he recalled. George Yeo, who was the Trade and Industry Minister, remembered it clearly. "It was always a problem justifying some of those things," he said, adding that he had approved Philip Yeo's move earlier. "But we had to move fast and the preference in any system is to, you know, be careful, assess risks. (But) someone must say look, okay, I'll take the risk, I'll bear the responsibility. We had to go through the process. Everybody along the process didn't want to take responsibility until he's convinced. And he's worried about the downside. So sometimes ... you have to be creative about the way you work the system to achieve your objective." But after some negotiation, when Philip Yeo agreed to let PSC have first dips on the scholarship applicants, he was allowed to proceed. "I agreed to let PSC interview the scholars first. And then they *chope*,[39] I don't touch them," he said. "We were looking at different groups anyway. The PSC offers bachelor degrees whereas I was giving out scholarships for PhD."

But trouble popped up again soon after. In 2005, Singaporean Chen Jiahao, who went by the online pseudonym of AcidFlask, made libellous remarks on his blog regarding A*STAR. A*STAR threatened legal action and Chen, a PhD student in University of Illinois-Urbana Champaign (UIUC), apologised and shut down his blog. But few knew the exact nature of the remarks. A*STAR did not want to point them out publicly so as to not repeat a libel. Unfortunately, it led many online to believe that A*STAR was bullying Chen because the latter was also questioning the high Grade Point Average (GPA) its scholars must achieve. As Nominated MP and technology lawyer Siew Kum Hong said in a media report, it looked like a "heavyweight" agency facing down a "poor student". The story even made it to the *Financial Times*.

183

Two years later, Chen's tussle with A*STAR would resurface. Yeo engaged Chen online and invited him to tea. Chen, who is a former PSC scholar, agreed but wanted to record the meeting in the presence of a third party and post it on his new blog. Yeo turned it down, telling *The Sunday Times*: "As I plan to visit UIUC, I thought I could invite him for tea on a one-to-one basis. Instead, he wanted to interrogate me with a witness and publish our meeting! Arrogant chap." During their online exchanges, Yeo brought up the 2005 defamation incident, prompting media queries on what exactly transpired in the original blog posts by Chen.

---

39   *Chope* is a colloquial term in Singapore which means "to reserve".

Yeo and A*STAR finally decided to tell the whole story, revealing for the first time that Chen had alleged that A*STAR bribed or offered incentives to get universities to accept its scholars. Yeo told *The Straits Times* in 2007: "The impression is that we forced him to take it (the blog) down. He is very sly ... very sneaky. I wish I had made everything public the first time." Independent observer Siew agreed that Chen had crossed the line. Chen's criticisms "went way beyond fair criticism as such, and alleged outright corruption by A*STAR in obtaining places for its scholars. This is a case where I can, and I think most unbiased and rational people would be able to, completely understand why A*STAR threatened legal action," said Siew.

Despite the controversies, the scholars are still Yeo's two-legged pride. He remained in touch with many and could still recite, sans notes, many of the scholars' schools, GPA, research interests and even choice of partners. "Look, this one, married an *ang moh*, but both came to Singapore to settle down," he said, using a local slang for Caucasian as he pointed to a wedding photo he had kept of a scholar. His long-time colleague Tan Chin Nam called his handling of the scholars "legendary". "It's very different from the PSC approach. It's a very personal approach. He was genuinely concerned with the progress of his scholars," he said.

Most of his scholars would agree. Former EDB and A*STAR scholar Ang Hwee Ching remembered Yeo not only encouraging her to pursue a PhD, but also introducing prominent scientists to her when they visited. "He would remember there's Hwee Ching who's interested in this particular topic and he would call me into his office and make an introduction," she said. "I have not come across anyone else like that who supported me so much in my career." Their association with Yeo often earned them both sympathy and

184

envy from friends. "They were envious because we got a chance to work with Chairman, who is larger than life," said former EDB scholar Jayson Goh. "They were sympathetic because they felt it could be quite *siong*[40] to work for him and if you can survive it, wow. We were always very proud to say that he actually took very good care of the team and the people working with him."

Yeo's talent development had an extra layer of shine, said Beh, because it went beyond the organisation that he was leading. "He's actually thinking about talent development for Singapore as a whole," he observed. "To give you an example, the A*STAR scholarships that he came up with wasn't just about scientific talent for A*STAR. He saw this as the pool of Singaporeans who would go on to lead the scientific endeavours in Singapore in the medium to long-term." It was the same with the EDB, with Yeo projecting that the scholars would leave public service and contribute to Singapore's economy in the private sector. "Few of us can emulate that, try as we might. It's not easy to think beyond the needs of your organisation," added Beh. "It's already very admirable that he's thinking 10, 15, 20 years ahead. But, in addition, he's thinking beyond the organisations that he's leading and he's thinking about talent development for Singapore as a whole."

185

---

40 *Siong* is a Hokkien word for "tough".

Q   *Why do you believe so strongly in scholarships as the way to go to get talent? Why not just employ the best talent from the market?*

A   I believe in catching them young and grooming them. The Spartans took the kid at seven years old and trained him to be a fighter. He was released from the military at 30. That's how Sparta became powerful despite only a population of 20,000. If you want to develop talent, you must start nurturing them from young.

Q   *Isn't that a form of social engineering?*

A   Yes. What's wrong with that? You don't get people by chance. I don't believe in chance.

Q   *That's a nanny state.*

A   I'm not mothering them. I'm selecting talent, I provide funding. I'm grooming people.

Q   *How did you arrive at the idea of slashing money from your research fund to create the scholarships at A*STAR?*

A   I don't know. It seems very natural to me. I don't know why others never thought of it.

Q   *You don't know why? Because only you can think of it. No one else would do it because it is something which they should not do!*

A   Yes, according to the rules. But my rule is when you have to beg, borrow or steal, the best option is to steal. You see, to beg is very humiliating. To borrow, you must return. Stealing is the best, as long as it is for the public good and not for personal gain. So I encourage my officers to steal.

Q   *You really didn't get anybody's approval for the scholarships?*

A   No.

Q   *Even the minister in charge didn't know?*

A   The minister was George Yeo, who was the Trade and Industry Minister. He didn't know. He found out when I asked him to give out the scholarships.

Q   *Wow, you're really quite the terror. Did you know it was illegal when you did it?*

A   I didn't care. That first batch of A*STAR scholars in 2001 are my "illegal scholars". For me, I was spending 100 per cent on research and at that point most of my researchers were foreigners. What was going on? I wanted the money for Singaporeans, to groom our own researchers.

Q   *So if you believe it is right, you are a person who would just do it?*

A   Yes, including stealing. I think public stealing for the public good is perfectly right. There's nothing wrong at all. Totally righteous. So as far as I'm concerned, I did not do anything wrong to take research funds for scholarships.

Q   *What do you look for in your scholars?*

A   The A*STAR scholarship is very expensive. For undergraduates, it cost us about S$300,000. The PhD is S$700,000. That's why I call them million-dollar kids. They cost a million bucks each. For such a hefty investment, I expect the best work from them. They must finish their undergraduate studies in three years with a minimum of 3.8 GPA. In the American system of grading, an A is 4.0 and an A- is 3.67. So if they managed to get half of the modules at A and the other half at A-, they will get an average of 3.8. What's the big deal?

Q   *Many have argued that it is too strict.*

A   Look, if they wanted to get into MIT or any top university, these schools would look at your grades. If they didn't have good grades, they wouldn't get into Stanford, MIT or Cambridge. I could fund them but the money wouldn't get them into these schools. Their grades would. I'm being elitist for their own sake.

Q   *What if they are bright but they didn't get 3.8?*

A   Wait, wait, wait. There are three years. Year 1, Year 2, Year 3. In the US, it is a cumulative system. So if you are smart, you make sure you got 4.0 in your first year, because that's when it is the easiest to score. Then 3.9 in your second year and 3.8 in your third. But if you screw up in your first year, it is hard to meet your target after that. There was a girl who joined a sorority in her first year in university and her grade was poor. She didn't manage to catch up. She didn't meet the 3.8 target. She withdrew and paid up the bond.

Q   *Some have said that the A*STAR scholars took easy modules so as to meet the 3.8 target.*

A   I look through all their transcripts every semester. If they did a lot of simple subjects and got straight As, it wouldn't fool me. Hey, it was taxpayers' money. I didn't take it lightly.

Q   *This part of you is quite surprising. Because you're a tinkerer, you're not somebody who sits down and writes papers. But yet for this, you insist that they do so well academically. Why?*

A   Academic results is a rough measure of the person's intellect. Otherwise, what other measures should I use? You go to MIT or Stanford, they also look at your scores, and they usually look for perfect scores. Of course, we also interviewed the person and observed them.

Q   *Grades may not get a future Philip Yeo.*

A   Well, I got 4As for A Levels, not bad. In my time, it was very hard to get 4As.

Q   *What happens when they want to drop out midway. Any bond breakers from A*STAR?*

A   They dropped out as undergrads because they realised they didn't want to pursue a PhD or they couldn't take it. I let them go. I remember a very bright girl who dropped out. She decided she didn't want to put in so many years to pursue a PhD. I transferred her to EDB. She served her bond there. To me, as long as they came home, and they worked in Singapore, I didn't complain. Or, if they tried for two, three years and they were unhappy, I said sure, go do something else that makes you happy.

Q *I don't understand. So you actually think it is okay to break bonds?*

A The most important thing to me is that they must have tried. At least they tried. When I was in EDB, the scholars came back and they were put on two years' probation. They were not confirmed. In the civil service they would have been confirmed after six months. I didn't do that in EDB. So after two years, if they couldn't fit in, I let them go. Either they bought out their bond or I transferred them to another agency which they wanted. To me, that's not bond breaking. You have tried, you cannot meet my standards or you are just plain unhappy, I let you go. I didn't want an unhappy scholar too. At A*STAR, we transferred scholars to private companies. There was a girl whom I transferred to Bayer. She served her bond there. They served out their bonds in major pharmaceutical firms in Singapore. As long as you continue to contribute to Singapore, I don't see that as breaking bond.

Q *I think very few people know that that's your definition of bond breaking.*

A I consider bond breakers those who didn't even try a single day. They graduate on a Friday in the US and tell you bye bye, I'm not coming home. You mean they couldn't even come back and try for one or two years? The government has paid for their education in full. The scholars whom we named were the ones who were not coming home to serve a single day. But as long as they return home to Singapore

190

and contribute, whether in A*STAR or EDB or a private firm, it's okay. My principle is very simple: we use taxpayers' money, so the scholars must come back to contribute, regardless of whether they do so in the public or private sector. It's very straightforward.

That's why I scolded Chng Hee Kok for encouraging people to break bonds. It's morally wrong. I mean, he broke his bond with PSC but he stayed in Singapore. I don't have a problem with that. But he refused to listen to my explanation and went to Parliament. It led to the huge hoo-ha in the newspapers, "Oh, Philip Yeo is a very wicked guy." Please. It wasn't my policy. It was the government's policy. It was signed off by the Deputy Prime Minister.

Q *Were you under a lot of stress during the Parliament debate?*

A I could not answer in Parliament. These MPs could have argued with me publicly. But they did it in Parliament and I could not be in Parliament to defend myself. I was very pissed off.

Q *Are you still pissed off after all these years?*

A Sure, I'm still pissed off! How could they do such things in Parliament? It was a Budget session for crying out loud and it was not related to the debate.

Q *How did you adjust your scholarship policies after that?*

A At A*STAR, every scholar signed a contract and their parents signed a separate letter to say they would not encourage their children to break the bond. Look, when you break your bond, who pays for it? It's the parents. So A*STAR scholarship is the only one which asks for family income and residential type. I didn't want rich kids who could afford to break bonds. When you are poor, you cannot break bonds. Who's going to pay for it? I didn't want them to waste my time. It's not the money. The money means nothing to me.

I took care of them for nine years through their PhD. I understand it is a great sacrifice for them to do their PhDs while their classmates were already out there working and getting good wages. So I gave the scholars a salary of more than S$3,000 a month when they were still pursuing their PhD. But I told them to save and not use the salary. They had overseas allowance, book allowance and their tuition paid for. Keep the salary aside and after five years, they would have about S$150,000 and could at least afford their downpayment for an HDB flat.

Q   *A criticism of the government scholarship scheme is that it offers a fast track for scholars and many do not spend enough time on the ground. What is your take?*

A   It is wrong. I don't believe in a fast track. As mentioned earlier, my EDB scholars were put on probation for two years. I don't know of any other statutory board which did that. To me, it was great that the scholars came back with a good degree from Imperial College or Cornell. But could he do the job? Their degrees meant nothing to me if they couldn't do the job. I gave them two years to prove themselves to me. We rated them every six months and if the ratings did not improve, we let them go after two years. I kept the good guys, I threw away the bad ones. If the guy couldn't fit, go somewhere else to serve out his bond. The joke was that I released them to TDB.[41]

---

41   TDB stands for Trade Development Board, the predecessor to International Enterprise Singapore, or IE Singapore, which promotes Singapore firms overseas and international trade.

Q   *Weren't you a beneficiary of a fast track in the civil service?*

A   There was no such thing as a fast track during my time. It was all up to the minister. If the minister moved you up fast, good for you. If not, *suay suay*,[42] too bad.

Q   *In some organisations, it is fairly common to see scholars leave the moment the bond is up. Some say that it's because they didn't know better when they took the scholarship at 18 years old and regretted their decisions. What is your view?*

A   If they leave the moment the bond is up, that means the company or organisation is not treating them well. It's down to how you manage talent.

   When I gave out scholarships, I kept in very close contact with them. I selected them and I monitored them. I asked for the results every quarter. I knew all of them and their families. I visited them every year at their universities. Do other chairmen and CEOs do that? Most do not. They leave it to others. When my scholars came home for holidays, they came to see me. There's nothing wrong with the scholarship system. It's how it is being implemented. It's how you manage people.

Q   *What do you think of bringing in foreigners to boost Singapore's talent pool?*

A   Singapore has always imported people. But in the last 10 years we imported too fast and too many. The tap was just turned on. The key is who do you bring in and how do you manage and assimilate

---

42 *Suay* means "unlucky" in the Hokkien dialect.

them. A persistent complaint is that our young fresh graduate has to compete with a fresh IT professional from India. What value can this new Indian guy bring to Singapore? If he is a senior person, okay, that's fine, because he is bringing his experience and knowledge and contacts. When I brought in the scientists, they were all top guys who could help our guppies. But a fresh foreign guy is just going to depress the Singaporean's wages. We should bring in foreign talent at the higher level and always to supplement, not to replace. The other group we should bring in are the really young ones, when they are still in school. Then they are more likely to assimilate and sink their roots here. Foreign talent must add to, and not subtract from, our people. They cannot displace our people.

As much as Yeo collected talent, he was also carefully curated and treasured by other patrons who shared a similar passion for the hobby. In his temple of talent saints, he named only two consistently: Goh Keng Swee and Lee Kuan Yew. And as Goh slid off because of poor health in the mid 1990s, Lee stepped in to offer Yeo the protection he needed as a chronic rule breaker. "Effectively, MM became the guy who looked out for Philip," said David Lim, referring to Lee by his last official title as Minister Mentor, or MM. "He ensured Philip had enough stature and resources to get things done."

The backing was critical. There were those in the highest echelons who did not view Yeo favourably. "When he was working with me, many of the Cabinet ministers didn't like his ways and really didn't feel he was suited for the service," said George Yeo. "I remember one night, when Lee Kuan Yew called me up to ask about what's happening ... and he was also very pained when he heard this (unhappiness among some leaders with Philip Yeo). So I said without him (Philip), many things could not be done. The whole effort in the biomedical sciences sector was largely (down to) him. Lee Kuan Yew said: 'I know he's sometimes insubordinate, but he's got great strengths, and it would be a great loss to Singapore (if) we were to lose him.' I completely agree."

When Yeo stepped down as chairman of A*STAR in March 2007, after the public spat with Lee Wei Ling on the future of Singapore's biomedical sciences push, he cited Lee Kuan Yew in his farewell speech. "Minister Mentor Lee Kuan Yew has asked me to reassure all of them (the whales and guppies). Let me quote MM Lee: 'This issue has been deliberated over a period of several months in Cabinet and decided by PM Goh and Cabinet. The policy has been continued by PM Lee and his Cabinet. We have made significant investments in time and resources. We have to get the most out of what we have put in.'"

The backing from Lee went beyond words. As Yeo once again toyed with the idea of leaving the civil service – his fifth and last failed escape attempt – he would be thwarted again by Lee, just like what happened in 2000, when Yeo was courted by Hong Kong tycoon Richard Li to join Pacific Century. After he left A*STAR in 2007, Lee asked him to be his Special Adviser on Economic Development, a newly-created role. "Lee Kuan Yew deliberately kept a place for him in PMO," said George Yeo, referring to the Prime Minister's Office. Philip Yeo would relinquish the job only when Lee retired from the Cabinet in 2011. "He asked me where I would work," recalled Yeo. "I told him: 'Don't worry, I have my own office.' Can you imagine me in the Istana?"

195

9

Memento Mori

*"You can have a visionary like Lee Kuan Yew
but somebody has to put it into practice.
Philip puts things to practice."*

Richard Sykes, honorary citizen of Singapore, former chairman of GlaxoSmithKline
and rector of Imperial College London, in a 2015 interview for this book

When a general returned in glory to ancient Rome after a successful battle, he was feted in a chariot-drawn procession through the streets. The spoils of his victory, the captives and the loot, led the way. His soldiers, in togas and laurel crowns, followed with chants of victory. The crowd applauded and the elite of the empire looked on admiringly. The general, on his four-horse chariot, was close to being a king for a day, a mortal on the cusp of divinity. But a slave accompanied the general through the procession, with only one duty, to whisper in the general's ears repeatedly: *"Memento mori* – remember, you will die."

The story may well be apocryphal, although its message of mortality and humility resonates. It certainly does for Philip Yeo. The Latin phrase is a favourite of his, a constant reminder against complacency. At every point when he reached the top, he looked for the downturn, a ceaseless journey across four decades of public service. It is almost a paradox. A civil servant who was always preparing for "turmoil" – his word – in a trade more commonly associated with stability and the iron rice bowl. But that explained his restless energy, best exemplified by his 5-5-5 rule on the temporal nature of industries – five years of initial struggles followed by five years of growth and finally five years of maturity and descent. David Lim summed up the Philip Yeo allergy to complacency: "When things are going very well, don't be too happy. When things are going really badly, don't be too depressed. That's life. We move in cycles." *Memento mori.*

Yeo rarely allowed himself the luxury of euphoria, relaxation or even contentment. A man of perpetual motion could not stand still or, worse, stop. Retirement is taboo. When close friend Lai Chun Loong, a long-time colleague in the defence industries, wanted to retire, he recalled Yeo exclaiming: "Do you want to die? If you don't work, you die!" A tad dramatic but Yeo practises what he preaches. Asked if he had considered retirement, he replied: "What do you want me to do? Die of boredom? Sit under the tree and become a buddha? I'll work until I can't walk."

While he eschews nirvana, his hunger for this-world fulfilment remains strong and his passion for Singapore undiminished. Every interview with him was both a memory project and a prospectus exercise of both the personal and the national. He looked back at his colourful career and friends pondered his legacy of leadership and management. But he could never take his eyes off the present and the future of Singapore, particularly in governance and economics. He has moved into the private sector, but public interests remain deeply important. Even as he sprints into the last laps of his life, taking it easy remains a phrase completely alien to the septuagenarian.

After he left A*STAR in 2007, then-Minister Mentor Lee Kuan Yew persuaded him to stay in the civil service as his Special Adviser on Economic Development. Yeo helped Lee when foreign countries sought advice on development. "Many countries, like Saudi Arabia, Russia and Kazakhstan, looked up to Mr Lee as a role model. My job was to help him help them, giving them advice on development," he said. When Lee travelled, Yeo would go along on some occasions, allowing him closer interaction with a leader whom he had worked with for decades but rarely had lengthy exchanges with. "We were not emotional people. We had short, effective meetings after which I would run off," said Yeo.

On a trip to Hanoi in 2009, Lee had lunch with Yeo along with others in the Singapore delegation. Lee's wife was not present, recalled Yeo, allowing the leader, who was known to be very careful with his diet, to be a little bit more adventurous with food. Yeo ordered *pho*, the popular Vietnamese noodle, and Lee was intrigued.

"What are you eating," he asked.

"Eating *pho*. Vietnamese noodle," replied Yeo. "You want some?"

"Okay."

Said Yeo: "He had a small bowl. I think it was the first time he had *pho*." After he had finished, Yeo asked him if he would like some dessert and recommended the restaurant's ice cream. Lee asked for two scoops – vanilla and chocolate. "Mrs Lee would never have allowed it," said Yeo with a gentle smile, holding on to a tender memory of the late leader who died in 2015. When Lee retired from the Cabinet in 2011, Yeo left his last official job with the authorities, except for a pro bono position as chairman of SPRING Singapore, an agency to help small and medium enterprises in Singapore prosper. He had a brief stint with Singbridge, a Temasek unit focused on China, before finally setting up his own business, Economic Development Innovations Singapore (EDIS), in 2013. He was 67.

The firm offers economic development services to foreign countries, with a focus on economic modelling and development as well as investment promotion. Not surprisingly, its main calling card is the brand of Philip Yeo. "There are many governments and investors around the world that are seeking practical advice and help on how to develop their economies and bring jobs to their locations," said EDIS executive director Abel Ang. "It is not difficult for an MBA, consultant, or economist to come up with a simple plan on what a location has unique competitive advantages for. It is quite another thing to go out and execute the plan and build an industry. Few people have the credibility that Philip Yeo has in being able to create so many different clusters of economic activity – IT, semiconductors, defence, chemicals, biomedical sciences, aerospace – in so many different geographies." EDIS has done work in countries ranging from Malaysia to Colombia, from Kazakhstan to Brazil. Said Yeo: "In a sense, I continue my expertise and it is surprising that there's quite a lot of demand. You know that old TV series *Have Gun – Will Travel*? That's me now. I'm a mercenary in ED," he added, before delivering his punchline with perfect standup comic timing. "Economic development, not erectile dysfunction."

His travel schedule remains punishing, partly because of his numerous directorships around the world. He sits on the boards of Kerry Logistics in Hong Kong, Hitachi in Japan, Baiterek National Management Holding in Kazakhstan and City Development and Accuron Technologies in Singapore, among others. It is not uncommon for a trip to include three continents, four time zones and five cities. His energy still surpasses many of his younger colleagues. "He is still decisive, quick thinking, and fast moving," said Ang. "However I think that to a certain extent, he has been confronted by his health and age and has to learn to adapt."

He struggles with the odd ailments on the road. On a visit to Colombia in 2015, he returned home with a severe bout of food poisoning. In other instances, his main bugbear these days is jet lag. "My stamina is fine, but it takes longer to recover from jet lag now," he said. "Lee Kuan Yew once asked me how I catch up with jet lag. I told him I slept on the plane. In the past, when I flew to the US, I would start work the moment I arrived there in the morning. The EDB guys were terrified of me. Now, I realise older people take longer to recover. I just came back from Frankfurt and Kazakhstan. Wow, took me a while to adjust."

As his work sinks deeper into the private sector and farther from Singapore, Yeo's public visibility in Singapore has receded significantly in the last few years. Gone are the days when he was as prominent as many senior politicians, a regular feature in the mainstream media. But when Singapore celebrated its 50th year of independence in 2015, months after Lee died, prompting bouts of introspection and concerns about the future, there had been calls for more mavericks like Philip Yeo. For instance, the Public Service Commission chairman Eddie Teo said in a speech in September 2015, a month after the jubilee celebrations of the nation, that the "public service ... needs a few mavericks like Philip Yeo. Enough to prevent groupthink, but not so many as to disrupt the institution".

The call was timely. Singapore has reached a level of economic development where there are few, if any, models to learn from. Emerging trends are new to the country, including an ageing population and a manpower-scarce economy. "We have not faced such challenges before," said Manpower Minister Lim Swee Say. At such a juncture, there is a need for a man like Yeo. "When you move a little bit to the left or to the right, that is not a problem. But when you go for a 90 degree turn, a big change, the system can feel uncomfortable. You need people who are prepared. One thing about Philip Yeo is that he never shies away from putting his neck on the chopping block. If he believes in something strongly enough, he's prepared to put his neck on the chopping block. But once he puts his head there, I can tell you, he will bulldoze through anybody who stands in his way. His philosophy is very simple: whose head is on this block? You will always need people like this."

The trick is knowing where to place such people in an organisation. While Yeo is a pathbreaker, he "doesn't do maintenance", observed EDB old boy Png Cheong Boon. It is a view shared by Sir David Lane. "He's brilliant at starting things but you know he's not the greatest at keeping it going," he said. To play to such strengths, it is critical to be strategic, said former Foreign Affairs Minister George Yeo. "You place individuals with different instincts in different parts of the organisation," he said. "You can't have a Philip Yeo type in some parts of civil service. It will not work. But where you're trying to break new ground, open new spaces, then you always need people like Philip Yeo." Former EDB managing director Ko Kheng Hwa agreed. He said: "More than ever before, we need creative and imaginative solutions, identifying opportunities and, equally important, the tenacity to implement things, to never give up. I think that's the reason why Singapore appreciates him more now. We need some thinking out of the box, take the path less beaten and dare to be different. The question is, how?"

A bunch of former colleagues turned friends had an idea. They started a programme at the NUS called the "Philip Yeo Initiative" in 2013, with an initial backing of S$5 million through matching government funds. It offers two types of awards. The first gives 10 students a chance to study and work overseas. It is an offshoot of an existing scholarship in the university. The second provides a grant of up to $20,000 for start-up projects. In 2014, a winner who designed his own wireless phone charging case was chosen, among others. The aim of the initiative is to inspire young Singaporeans with some Philip Yeo spirit. Besides providing money, Yeo meets the winners and provides contacts around the world, opening doors for the young folks.

The maverick can't be recreated, acknowledged those behind the scheme – a small band of Yeo supporters who call themselves "Mad Cows" – an acronym for "Making a Difference, Changing Our World". Nobel laureate Sydney Brenner, a close friend, said as much. "I don't think you can clone such a person. He is unique," he said. But some of his ingenuity and leadership skills can be passed on. "His brand of leadership is unique. He dares to push boundaries and to do what's right, not for himself, but for the nation," said National Gallery chief Chong Siak Ching, who was one of those behind the idea, at the launch of the initiative. Added Lim Swee Say, who was also present: "We cannot duplicate Philip Yeo, but the least we can do is to spread this Philip Yeo spirit, this Philip Yeo culture, and most importantly the Philip Yeo passion."

Some of this spirit, culture and passion have already spread through the civil service, among those whom he had worked with. Said former JTC chairman Lim Neo Chian: "Many of the people who worked with him, and some of them are still around, would have been very much influenced by his style of working. At EDB, for example, his imprint is still there. A lot of people there used to work for Philip Yeo. And to these younger lot of

202

people, Philip Yeo is like god." Indeed, current EDB chairman Beh Swan Gin said Yeo's influence in the organisation remains deep even though it has been nearly a decade since he left. "Look, he was chairman for 15 years and then co-chairman for another five. So his influence on EDB's culture is incredible," said Beh. "And all of us who are in senior management today were young officers when he was chairman. Whether it is about a can-do spirit, whether it's about integrity issues, whether it's about being bold and being imaginative, we will literally quote things that he said. I mean, things like 'easier to ask for forgiveness than to ask for permission' and stuff like this. These are all stories from Philip Yeo."

It is no coincidence that when this author wrote to several of the EDB mafia, the e-mail replies were like Yeo's – almost instantaneous and in short bursts of staccato sentences. One of them was current EDB managing director Yeoh Keat Chuan. He said: "Quite frankly, it's much easier to write long, lengthy paragraphs than it is to write short because it requires you to have clarity of thinking. His (Yeo's) replies are usually two sentences. If he writes a lot, you know you're in trouble." Speed of response was also shaped by him, added Yeoh. "I remember one incident where he had sent us an e-mail asking for inputs. Out of five of us, four replied within 12 hours. The one poor guy said 'oh my computer was down,' and so replied only after 48 hours. Chairman replied: 'Well, we have already decided. And secondly, you should throw your computer out of the window because we are not paying you so much to have computers that don't work. You should get your computer working.' Speed represents that whole customer-centricity, to be able to respond, because in the private sector, clearly, if you need to move, you need to move. You react to that pace."

A few traits of Yeo's leadership were consistently mentioned: decisive, quick, and, surprisingly, compassionate. He and his Mad Cows referred to it as "kite-flying" leadership, a phrase first used by Lim Swee Say. "To get the best out of people, don't be paternalistic. You have to treat them like kites," said Yeo at the launch of the Philip Yeo Initiative. "You get them up in the air, if there's no wind you try again. Everybody needs a lift-off. If they get into trouble, you reel them in." Clearly, the talent hunter not only reeled in the people he wanted, but also retained and nurtured them.

There are five key characteristics of the "kite-flying" leadership. First, he detested micromanagement. He let the kite fly. Almost every one of his former staff talked extensively about the space which Yeo gave them, including the most junior officers, to operate. "He let you loose," said Lim Swee Say. "As young officers, we actually felt very motivated by this style of leadership because we had a chance to think of our own way and work out our own solution." Former EDB managing director Tan Chin Nam agreed. "Philip Yeo, as the overall leader, was able to empower the staff," he shared. "You get a lot of flexibility, a lot of freedom to do what you want. I must say I really enjoyed working with him." It is true for his secretary too. Mary Chan, who has been working with Yeo for two decades, said she is allowed to shape her work. "He won't say 'you must do this and that,'" she shared. "I use my initiative to decide how to get things done. I like it. He gives me a platform to be exposed to different things, to excel and to learn to be more resourceful."

The antipathy towards micromanagement has its roots in Goh Keng Swee's management handbook, said Yeo, which emphasises delegation with oversight. He said: "I don't like people to breathe down my neck, so I don't breathe down my staff's necks." One of his favourite sayings is: "If I have to tell you how to do it, I might as well do it myself." When he was running the Singapore Technologies (ST) group as exco chairman, the chiefs of subsidiary firms saw him every Saturday and only if they wanted to. Lai, who was president of Chartered Industries of Singapore (CIS), said: "When you built up the trust and relationship with him that you could deliver, he would give you a lot of room to work. He would not micromanage you. He had so many other jobs on his plate. He didn't have the time to go through the nitty gritty." It was the same at home, said his son Eugene. "I think a lot of parents, especially Singaporean parents, like to tell their kids what to do with their lives. He's never really done that," he said. "He gives you a very long rope to hang yourself – very, very long. He's not a micromanager and I think that's clear from his professional life."

Somewhat surprisingly, several former colleagues said Yeo was patient with his kites. Former EDB officer Jonathan Kua shared: "He was impatient at work and yet patient when dealing with the staff. He had a persona that was very different from his public image. For 99 per cent of the time, he was charging ahead. But after every battle, he would explain patiently with a tenderness most people did not see." Lim Swee Say distilled Yeo's management to one word: why. "He was interested only in the 'why'," he explained. "He would tell you why this needed to be done. But he will leave you to figure out how to do it and what needs to be done."

Second, he demanded responsibility and ownership. In fact, he relished it, preferring to lead from the front and on the ground. Once, despite injuring his ankle, he persisted with a trip to the US. "We landed in Detriot and although he was clearly in pain, he walked a very long 40 minutes in the airport with his suitcase," said current EDB director of human resource Ng

Ying Yuan. "He refused any help. He wanted to show us that he was there with the troops."

He was the kite flyer and he left no one in any doubt of his leadership status. "There are people who try to get by without being clearly accountable for things, so that if things go wrong, they are not accountable," observed Lim Neo Chian. "But Philip Yeo was quite different. He took on things if he thought they were important. Even when things were not his business, but if they might impact his ability to get things done, he would go there to influence the results. He didn't mind taking on responsibility and making things happen. It also meant that if things went wrong, his head was on the chopping board. He didn't mind. He would tell you: 'Sack me! If you're not happy, you sack me!'."

The ownership he imposed was especially important given his habit of breaking rules within the strait-laced civil service. Said Lim Swee Say: "When he broke the rules, he also took ownership. The worst type of rule breakers are the ones who run away once something goes wrong. That's not Philip Yeo. He stood by his decisions and no matter how powerful the critics, he was unmoved. He had never put the blame on his people, not even once. He provided the cover." Critically, he would remain loyal to the subordinates. Said Senior Minister of State Josephine Teo, an EDB alumnus: "When you work for Philip Yeo, you are never going to be left in the lurch. If you have done an honest job, if you've tried your damndest and things did not go quite as planned, he's not going to come from behind and say, 'Oh you didn't do this?' He's not that kind of despicable person. He backs you 100 per cent, all the way." That translated into a team of strong fighters, said Tan Chin Nam, brimming with confidence. "He always backed his staff. I believe that gave his staff a lot of confidence, knowing that the boss had your back," he said.

Third, Yeo preferred to deal directly with staff, even those at the lowest level. Nothing comes between him and his kites. At CIS, he would reach the factory early in the morning and walked the floor to speak to the technicians and machinists. "He liked to see the shop floor," recalled Lai. Said Yeo, "I listened to the workers and they would tell me their problems. Most managers go into the office, sit down and put their legs up. I learnt from Dr Goh. He visited a battalion every week. That kept the commanders on their toes." He bypassed most proper channels to connect with the ground directly. Said John Wong: "He takes a genuine interest in people. He's not someone who believes in either titles or hierarchy." During Yeo's time in EDB, he was accompanied on every trip by a different young staffer. This allowed him to "inspire the young officer of the vision and task, and he got to know the officer fairly well too", said Ko. "And by getting to know them, I do not mean just through work. He often also got to know about their families and their personal lives."

The personal touch, said many former EDB alumni, was an integral, albeit unexpected, aspect of Yeo's leadership. He formed emotional attachments to his colleagues in a way few leaders could, or bothered to, stretching across the spectrum of an organisation. When his best friend, Wong Kok Siew, died suddenly in 2005 after suffering a stroke, he took out a personal obituary to pay tribute to his former classmate and right-hand man in Mindef, ST group and Sembcorp. "Suddenly, I have lost Wong Kok Siew, my closest buddy and colleague. His loss leaves me with a pain and a void beyond words of mere sorrow," he wrote. When his secretary's mother died, he asked someone to take over a work presentation so that he could attend the wake. "Even though I was only a secretary, he went the extra mile," said Mary Chan. Former EDB director Khoo Seok Lin called him a "relational leader". She shared: "Once, he called me to his office and took out two Star Wars comic books. He told me his daughter loved it and he could find it only in London. He got some for her and some for my son, who was a year older than his daughter. From that day onwards, I would do whatever he wanted me to do. He did not see me as a piece of asset, as a director of human resource. He saw me as a mother and he even remembered my son's name. That's how he was as a leader."

While on a trip in San Francisco to study the biomedical sciences industry, NUS president Tan Chorh Chuan remembered Yeo's attention not only to senior staff, but also to junior officers. "One of the officers had, for some reason, not enough shirts," he said. "Philip Yeo went and bought a couple of shirts for that person. He did it without any fuss." When Yeo noticed that Wong's presentations were in black and white, he bought him a colour printer. "No civil servant has ever sent me a printer," said Wong. As Wong travelled the world to hunt for "whales", Yeo gave him a Nokia – his first mobile phone. "Philip genuinely wanted to try and make my life easier," he said. At times, Yeo's intimate connection even went beyond the human touch. Said Png: "He would meet up with those of us in EDB based overseas whenever he was in town. He would ask 'how's the family, how's the wife doing, how are the kids doing?' In fact, those days we had a dog, so he asked, 'how's the dog doing?'."

Thanks to technology, Yeo could maintain the personal connection with his staff, scholars and friends. He is known as a one-man news agency, sending articles to his network of contacts through e-mails. "He will send me all kinds of articles ... too many things," said George Yeo. "So I read some of them and the rest I diligently file away, hoping to read them when I have more time. But I never find more time. He's like a broadcaster, you see." The topics are wide-ranging. Said David Lim: "He copies folks on what he thinks they might be interested in and perhaps what he wants them to know. Sometimes controversial viewpoints, other times just science or Op-Eds. Once in a while, a personal thing or two. I think it's a great way to stay connected and poll for views. That's his way of keeping abreast of things, other than just reading ... he gets reactions!" The Philip Yeo news service offers customised content too. "I often receive articles from him – about the latest thinking and innovations in my area of work – business park or science park developments – when I was in Ascendas," said Chong Siak Ching. "As soon as I switched to the National Gallery role, I was receiving articles about museums and the arts! He is always connecting ideas to people, and people to people."

209

Fourth, as long as results were achieved, Yeo was not one who obsessed over the methods. "Get the job done," he said. Just fly the damn kite. Said Tan Chin Nam: "He wanted to act fast ... we couldn't think and think forever, and have no action. Philip Yeo couldn't tolerate that." To reach the goals, he quite readily embraced imperfections. Said Lim Swee Say: "His philosophy is – you must be prepared to live with someone's weakness in order to have access to his strength. But you'd better have some strengths that could help him to achieve what he wanted. If he came to the conclusion that you had no relevant strengths, then he would let you go. There are people who had so much nonsense that they could not survive elsewhere. But they thrived under Philip Yeo. Why? Because Philip Yeo focused on their strength, not their weakness."

Josephine Teo, who was the EDB and A*STAR human resource director, said her former boss had a "high degree of tolerance for talent". "He knew that there were some brilliant people who were rude, he knew that there were some brilliant people who didn't play by the rules, who did not want the same sets of conditions to apply to them, he understood that," she said, laughing at the recollection. "He understood that talent demands special treatment. He was very willing to accommodate their desires within what was reasonable. He wanted me to let everyone have special treatment. Everyone was special. He has a great tolerance for prima donnas, yes. And there were so many prima donnas because they knew that he would put up with them!" Not that he was completely indulgent. While he would rescue his staff when mistakes were made, a severe tongue lashing would follow. Said Lim: "When we got into trouble, he would rescue us. But once you got out of trouble, he would scold you. How bad? When he was angry, he was really angry. Your face would turn pale." Yeo had a three strikes rule, allowing for three different mistakes. He said: "If you make the same bloody mistake, then you must be really stupid."

Last, while Yeo has a surprising caring touch, his leadership carries an uncompromising edge in which he was not afraid to let the kite go. He called it his "Black September" – an annual culling of poor performing staff. "You must make it a habit of firing a few people, then everybody would be on their toes," he said. "Everywhere I went, the first people I fired were the managers. I never fire the workers. It's not the fault of the workers. Whenever a company has problems, it is because of problems in management. When people feel they are being taken care of, that they're being recognised, and when workers respect their bosses and are able to work with minimum interference, their productivity will be unlimited. People don't work for pay alone. People work because they are recognised and valued. They leave a company because they don't feel wanted."

When mistakes were serious, the kite would be discarded. Said Goh Song How, who worked closely with Yeo on the Batam project: "He'll say, get rid of this guy. That's how strict he can be." At CIS, he sacked the human resource manager because of persistent high staff turnover. "HR was separate from the plant. Every time the factory lost a worker, HR simply took out an advertisement and hired a new person. The loss meant nothing to them," he recalled. "I sacked the manager and made the plant manager double as HR. I told him that every worker whom we lost, I would charge the recruitment cost to the plant. HR quickly realised that they had better be nice to the workers." Lai concurred. "He likes to line them up and shoot them," he said.

But others said the legend of Philip Yeo's Black September has been somewhat exaggerated. "Of course you hear many stories about how he can be very demanding. And I don't think that is incorrect," said Yeoh Keat Chuan. "He wouldn't be where he is with his track record if his people could not execute what needed to be done. I know of one case where the officer accompanying him on a trip didn't perform up to the standards and was sent home. These stories propagate. But by and large, in 90 per cent of the cases, he had no problems with his subordinates." Teo agreed. "I didn't find him that demanding. All he expected of you was to apply your mind to what he asked you to do and give him the best possible analysis that you could, then give him the best possible course of action and do it. When you have a boss that is that clear, it actually is not very difficult," she said. "He gives you a very long leash, just don't use it to hang yourself."

Q   *What is the rationale behind your firing-squad approach to managers?*

A   Like Dr Goh, I don't believe people can change. So the best way to change an organisation is to burn it down and start afresh. That means I sack the whole lot of managers. In every organisation, there are three types of people: the emperors at the top, the workers at the bottom and the eunuchs in the middle. The ruler says, "I want my pyramid," and the workers are the people who built it. The eunuchs are the ones who shuffle papers. They don't do any real work. Their objectives are to keep the emperor happy. How to do that? Keep the emperor entertained or distract him with other preoccupations. Eunuchs destroy empires. It was true in China and also in the West. The Ottoman Empire was brought down by eunuchs too. All they did was create problems between the emperors and the commanders who did real work out in the battlefields. All they did was play palace politics.

Q   *Who are the eunuchs in the Singapore context?*

A   We call them "staffers". I advise CEOs and top civil servants to go into the field, visit the companies and spend time with the workers. But many still prefer to hold meetings and presentations. They create another layer and it is a layer filled with staffers. Soon, the leader will be infected with eunuch disease.

Q   *What is eunuch disease?*

A   It is when a leader surrounds himself with staffers and he becomes increasingly isolated. It is a common cancer in pyramidal organisations. The best organisation structure is flat. If I'm the emperor, I would want to see the generals myself. I would command the generals. I would not leave it to another tier. Increasingly, the emperors in Singapore do not see their generals because there are so many layers.

Q *How did Singapore get to this stage? Is it because as society becomes more developed, it requires a more complex governance structure?*

A No, it's how the leadership has evolved. Now, everywhere you go, the leaders have so many staffers. There are so many papers which need to be submitted, and then summarised for the management. Why can't the leader read the paper himself? The paper should not be long. Why is there a need to write a long damn paper? Who's going to read it? Dr Goh used to demand that a paper is no longer than one page and it must be written in simple English. He always said: short and sharp. If you cannot tell me in one page or in five minutes, it means you have no clarity of thought. I have no patience because a damn idiot wants to write his grandmother's story. Some of the leaders have this bad habit today. They like to ask for long papers – writing diarrhoea. Leaders should demand clarity instead of this paper-generating culture.

Q *Is this a result of how talent is recruited?*

A The organisation wants stability. There must be a balance with some turmoil. If it is all stability, it gets really boring and a maverick won't want it. He will run away. You will get people who are honest and respectable, but you won't get mavericks. These are the people who follow rules – "Yes, Sir, I will do this." They are your obedient kids in schools and teachers like them. They grow up to be good eunuchs. They sit down and don't move around. They are better than the guy who cannot sit still, the kind who has an itchy backside and will get into trouble. I used to get into trouble in school. I finished my work fast and I made noise in class. The teacher made me stand at the blackboard. I'm happy to stand. Better than sitting in the stupid chair.

Q *How much of this increasing bureaucratisation is seen in Singapore today?*

A The management is too involved in day-to-day matters. They become administrators rather than leaders. Let me tell you a story. When Lee Kuan Yew was in charge, he called me to Istana one day. He was still Prime Minister and I was EDB chairman. I sat down. It was just the two of us.

214

"Can you bring investments to Woodlands?" he asked me.

"Can you put an MRT station there?" I replied.

Finished. I walked out. Our conversation lasted less than a minute. I knew he called the Minister of Communications right away and said that Woodlands must get an MRT station. I quickly got TECH – Texas Instruments, EDB, Canon and Hewlett Packard – Semiconductors to get set up in Woodlands, way before the MRT station was even up. I pushed for projects to go to Woodlands. I didn't write a memo. I didn't have to answer him on how we were going to do it. He took my word and I took his word. He wanted something and I delivered.

Today, ministers overwork – doing everything and appearing everywhere. When there were issues with CPF,[43] the minister answered. Where was the CPF chairman? When the trains broke down, the minister answered. Where was the SMRT chairman? In

---

43 CPF is an acronym for Central Provident Fund – Singapore's national pension fund.

the past, the civil servants would take charge. Sim Kee Boon would tell Ong Teng Cheong,[44] "Minister, leave it to me." When I was second permanent secretary at Mindef, there was a big fire at a Bukit Timah ammunition depot. I told the minister that I would take care of it.

Now, the Admin Officers[45] are quiet. That is a sad thing. In my time, permanent secretaries were permanent in their postings. Today, we should call them "temporary secretaries" because they get rotated every few years. There's no reservoir of experience. I was in Mindef for almost 15 years and I remained in the defence industries for another eight years. More than 20 years in total in defence. Now, all the AOs are assistant director, then deputy director, shuffled from ministry to ministry with no domain knowledge. It's not their fault. They are well-educated. But they are constantly rotated and they have no depth.

Q *How does this contrast with the Old Guard leaders?*

A The Old Guards were politicians. They built a nation from next to nothing. They didn't care about the nitty gritty. Just get the bloody job done. Bring in investments, create jobs, build up an army. They didn't have time to discuss with you "on the one hand and on the other hand". They sketched the big picture, they told you what they wanted and they left you alone to do it. It's based on trust. When Lee Kuan Yew asked me to consider being his special adviser in 2007, he said to me: "Philip, your problem is that the older generation of leaders value you. The younger generation does not." I replied that I knew that and was happy to work for him. I'm very fussy about my bosses. I had only three real bosses in my career – Dr Goh, Howe Yoon Chong and LKY. In Oct 2006, then 83-year-old Howe Yoon Chong hosted a 60th birthday private lunch for me in his Straits

---

44 The late Sim Kee Boon was a former head of civil service. The late Ong Teng Cheong was a former deputy prime minister and later elected president of Singapore.
45 Administrative Officers (AOs) are part of the Administrative Service, the elite ranks of the Singapore civil service.

Trading Company office with his favourite rich Penang food. It was most memorable.[46]

Q   *Did you ever consider joining politics?*

A   Howe Yoon Chong and Sim Kee Boon asked if I would be interested. This was in the 80s. I laughed. I told them "Mr Howe, you already complained to me about being a politician and you still want me to join you?" Sim Kee Boon laughed. You see, Howe Yoon Chong had complained to us many times that he felt like strangling his residents sometimes because of their very unreasonable requests. He said one of them said he wouldn't vote for the PAP if he couldn't get a social visit pass for his foreign wife. Howe had a temper you know?

So anyway, I told him my personality would never be suited for politics. I can't imagine me being nice to my voters. I would probably strangle them. When I run an organisation, I don't need to ask for your vote. That's the freedom I have. I can't see myself as a politician. What I wanted to do was to go into the business world.

Q   *Do you think Singapore can remain exceptional?*

A   It depends on exceptional people who're willing to serve. It's up to the present leadership and the future generation. I'm concerned about Singapore's economy. What's the next engine of our growth? Is it tourism? But do you create good jobs with tourism? You don't need highly-qualified people. All you need is a tour guide. Look at Formula One. For a few days, all the chauffeured cars and the hotels are occupied. It's like the Singapore Airshow. It's a one-week event and the tourists leave after that. These are not sustainable, everyday industries. These are icing on the cake.

216

---

46 Howe Yoon Chong passed away in August 2007.

When you have mass unemployment, tourism is good to create a lot of jobs. But they are not high value jobs. In the hotel industry, most of the jobs are very labour intensive, like chambermaids, cleaners and waiters. No one has invented a bed that can clean by itself. Except for the hotel manager, these workers do not need a university education. So do we want our younger Singaporeans to aspire to such jobs? In America, they are called hamburger flippers. They do the McDonald's, KFC, Subway kind of very low-skilled job with low wages.

So far, I haven't seen anything new that can create good and sustainable jobs. After biomedical sciences, what's next? Space? Some years ago, EDB had a "Home" strategy to get companies to deepen their relationship with Singapore. I liked to joke with them that they should call it "Home Alone", like the movie. Why Home? Is Singapore now into hospitality? Will that draw new investors? When I was promoting industries, we moved from data storage to semiconductors to chemicals and then to biomedical sciences. Every few years, there was a new fashion, just like in clothing. It was a fashion statement. Now, there doesn't seem to be a new fashion. What are we selling to our young people? What's the new dream? It is a harder job today for EDB. But we must keep trying.

Q
&
A

217

Q   *How do you think you will be remembered in Singapore?*

A   Not my problem.

For a man who continues to divide opinions years after he has slipped out of the public eye, his legacy is likely to be a controversial one. There are many who continue to regard him as an arrogant and uncompromising bureaucrat, who was, in his word, "evil". But there are also those who look up to him as a daredevil maverick who did genuine work for Singapore, creating good jobs and not afraid to speak his mind. Sir David Lane referred to him as "one of Singapore's greatest leaders". The debate is unlikely to cease anytime soon.

But some chapters of his story are indisputable. His contributions in defence, the economy and talent development are clear success stories in the larger narrative of Singapore's journey from Third World to First. In these areas, his impact was "very significant", said Lim Neo Chian. "He went in and really set the pace, defined the vision, and drove it. He has left a big imprint and influenced a lot of people." In particular, the talent he groomed stood at the top of the list, an achievement he has been most proud of. The most prominent ones include George Yeo, Lim Swee Say, David Lim, Josephine Teo, Lee Yi Shyan, Tan Chin Nam, Beh Swan Gin, Yeoh Keat Chuan and Png Cheong Boon. "He would be remembered as somebody who had that talent focus and nurtured large numbers of very talented people who have then gone on to contribute in very important ways in Singapore," said Tan Chorh Chuan. "And in the end, talent is the single most important thing that you can contribute."

Singaporeans ought to be grateful for his work, said Richard Sykes, former CEO of GlaxoSmithKline and rector of Imperial College London. "Without him, Singapore would be worse off. Singaporeans should really thank Philip Yeo because I think he did a tremendous amount for the country both economically and socially. He was one of the great developers of the country. You can have a visionary like Lee Kuan Yew but somebody has to put it into practice. Philip puts things to practice. Philip was a doer and you needed doers, particularly in developing economies." The alternative would be much slower growth, said Tan Chin Nam. "Without him bulldozing through, I think you may not be able to achieve progress," he observed. "I think it's better to have progress than to sit around doing nothing." Or in the words of John Wong, he was "Singapore's magic weapon". "If you want to create something from nothing, get Philip Yeo," he said.

Above all, he was a patriot. From bullets to missiles, from jobs to scholarships, Yeo's consistency ran through more than four decades of public service. It was always about his fellow men – to defend them, to feed them and to ensure those who have benefited would remain in the island to perpetuate a virtuous circle of unbroken peace and prosperity. "He's fiercely loyal and patriotic to Singapore," said Wong. It is a tad cliched, but the interests of the country are the most important to him, according to almost every single one interviewed in the writing of this book. "He wants to do the best thing for Singapore. Philip Yeo took immense pride in being a Singaporean," added Lim Swee Say. "So he's always thinking about the future of Singapore – what is going to happen. A truly amazing man, full of ideas. But whatever ideas he came up with, whatever rules he broke, it was all for a clear purpose. He did not break rules for the fun of breaking rules. He did not come up with ideas for the fun of coming up with ideas. He dared to be different not because he just wanted to be different, but because he was guided by a very singular purpose; he wanted Singapore to continue to do well."

For the man himself, a look back at his 40 years in public service threw up surprisingly simple life lessons. In a speech to NUS students at a commencement ceremony in 2011, when he was conferred an Honorary Doctor of Letters, he said: "As I look back on my career, what have been memorable for me are not the achievements. Neither are the advancements. What has been memorable is the fun I have had in all the jobs I have held! What is fulfilling to see is what new opportunities my work has generated for others. Finally, the friendships I have built along the way have made it an enjoyable journey! That is what lasts.

"In short, my advice to you is if you do what you love, create opportunities for others and boldly make new friends, you will certainly succeed and be happy." The pursuit of such joys goes some way to understanding the man behind the maverick and the secret of his success. It is about passion, purpose and people. Posterity holds little significance for the simple man called upon to achieve big things during exciting times. The riddle of Philip Yeo will live on, an exercise in historical analysis for future generations of Singaporeans. He has only one request: "Don't ever call me a civil servant. I was neither civil nor servant."

ACHIEVEMENTS
& AWARDS

1974	Awarded the Singapore Public Administration Medal (Silver)
1982	Awarded the Public Administration Medal (Gold)
1991	Awarded the Meritorious Service Medal
1994	Awarded the Indonesian Government conferred - highest civilian honour, the Bintang Jasa Utama (the First Class Order of Service Award) in recognition of his role in fostering good bilateral ties between Indonesia and Singapore.
1996	Conferred the Order National du Merite (National Order of Merit) for his contribution and leadership in enhancing ties between Singapore and France.
June 1997	Conferred the honorary Doctor of Engineering by University of Toronto, Canada
Feb 1998	Honoured by the Belgium Government with the Commander of the Belgium National Order of the Crown for his personal merits in promoting the cooperation between Belgian and Singapore industries.
Nov 1998	Honoured by the International Society of Design and Process Science with the K T Li Award of Taiwan for contributing significantly to economic and societal development.

2003	Awarded the CEO Lifetime Achievement Award, Asia Pacific IPA Awards
May 2006	Conferred the honorary Doctor of Medicine by Karolinska Institutet, the foremost medical school in Sweden.
2006	Awarded the Order of Nila Utama, First Class (Darjah Utama Nila Utama), one of Singapore's most prestigious National Day Awards
May 2006	Received the Japan Nikkei Prize for Science and Technology "in honor of his strong leadership in drafting and implementing Singapore's science and technology strategy, particularly in biomedical sciences."
Sept 2006	Received the Harvard Business School's Alumni Achievement Award. Harvard credits him with moving Singapore's economy into manufacturing sectors such as disk drives, semiconductors, petrochemicals, and biomedical sciences.
Nov 2007	Conferred the honorary Doctor of Science by Imperial College London for being one of "Singapore's true pioneers of economic development in harnessing Singapore's skills in industries such as semiconductors, aerospace, specialty chemicals and biomedical sciences".
Dec 2007	Conferred the Order of the Rising Sun, Gold and Silver Star by the Japanese Government.

May 2008 ○ Awarded the Distinguished Service (Star) award by the Singapore's Labour Movement, National Trade Unions Congress, for his contributions to the transformation of Singapore's economic landscape and creating the conditions of Singaporeans to enjoy more and better job opportunities. The award is the Singapore Union's highest honor for a non-unionist.

Nov 2008 ○ Awarded the University of Toronto Engineering Alumni Medal

Mar 2009 ○ Awarded the "1st BioSpectrum Asia-Pacific Life Time Achievement Award" for efforts in making Singapore one of the most exciting BioScience hub through a variety of policy, fiscal measures and setting up of world class infrastructure.

July 2011 ○ Conferred the honorary Doctor of Letters by National University of Singapore.

Nov 2011 ○ Conferred the honorary Doctor of Law by Monash University of Australia.

May 2014 ○ Awarded the 2014 Distinguished Alumnus Award by Eisenhower Fellowships in recognition of leadership in the Eisenhower Fellowships alumni network; and post-fellowship activities that have reflected President Eisenhower's commitment to peace and productivity by working through direct personal contacts across boundaries.

ACKNOWLEDGEMENTS

It took his close friends and colleagues nearly 10 years to convince Philip Yeo that a biography is a worthwhile project, one which could offer useful lessons to Singaporeans, especially the younger generation, of the challenges of building a nation. As is typical of the man, the moment he agreed and gave his word, he devoted 100 per cent support to it. He gave me unprecedented access to his time, space and memories. Nothing was off limits as he generously shared from his cavernous library and e-mail servers dating back several decades. He opened up his personal archives of letters, documents and e-mails, including some which showed him in a less than flattering light. Even though he was clearly uncomfortable sharing his private life, he made an effort to do so. I am most grateful to him and his family for their patience and cooperation. A biographer cannot ask for more.

But as Philip Yeo himself would say over and over again during our interviews, none of his achievements was accomplished by him alone. His strength has always been the ability to gather a capable team to get the job done. In the writing of this book, I benefited from having such a group of wise men and women to bounce off ideas and improve the product. David Lim, Khoo Seok Lin and Abel Ang were an informal council of advisers whom I relied on heavily to fill in the gaps in the Philip Yeo story. Their insights were invaluable. Ivan Choong walked the distance with me. He was my partner at many interviews, and contributed significantly through his meticulous research.

I am heavily indebted to Han Fook Kwang. He brought me into this project, guided me through the process and was always available to help me untangle narrative knots. In a style reminiscent of Philip Yeo's management, Fook Kwang gave me plenty of room to explore and experiment and I am most thankful for his gentle guidance and kindness.

This is the third book I am writing with Straits Times Press and the hat trick is testament to the level of comfort I have with the professional team led by Susan Long. It is always a joy working with talented people with a strong passion in words, design and books. I have enjoyed collaborating with Audrey Yow, Lock Hong Liang, Ilangoh Thanabalan and Fong Siew Chong.

Finally, every author knows that writing is a lonely and, at times, painful process. But my journey through the production of this book has been made easier because of a supportive family. My parents gave unquestioning love which I treasure more each day as I embrace parenthood myself. My sisters and their families always had my back and made sure my feet stayed on the ground. My in-laws were quiet cheerleaders who gave me ample encouragement. My wife Sue-Ann is the rock of my life and enjoyed the many stories which I shared with her while writing this book. It is my hope that the drive, imagination and kindness of Philip Yeo will inspire our boys Joshua, Edward and Micah, instilling in them an entrepreneurial streak laced with generosity and patriotism.

Peh Shing Huei